The
Biblical Basis
for the
Papacy

The
Biblical Basis
for the
Papacy

John Salza

Our Sunday Visitor Publishing Division
Our Sunday Visitor, Inc.
Huntington, Indiana 46750

Nihil Obstat: Rev. Michael Heintz
Censor Librorum

Imprimatur: ✠ John M. D'Arcy
Bishop of Fort Wayne-South Bend
October 20, 2006

The *Nihil Obstat* and *Imprimatur* are official declarations that a book or
pamphlet is free from doctrinal or moral error. It is not implied that those who
have granted the *Nihil Obstat* and *Imprimatur* agree with the contents,
opinions, or statements expressed.

Unless stated otherwise, Scripture citations used in this work are from the
Douay-Rheims version of the Bible. Other Scripture citations are from the
Catholic Edition of the Revised Standard Version of the Bible (RSV-CE),
copyright © 1965 and 1966 by the Division of Christian Education of the
National Council of the Churches of Christ in the United States of America.
Used by permission. All rights reserved.

Every reasonable effort has been made to determine copyright holders of
excerpted materials and to secure permissions as needed. If any copyrighted
materials have been inadvertently used in this work without proper credit
being given in one form or another, please notify Our Sunday Visitor in
writing so that future printings of this work may be corrected accordingly.

Our Sunday Visitor Publishing Division
Our Sunday Visitor, Inc.
200 Noll Plaza
Huntington, IN 46750

ISBN: 978-1-59276-284-2 (Inventory No. T373)
LCCN: 2006940662

Cover design by Tyler Ottinger
Cover art: Angus Images
Interior design by Sherri L. Hoffman

PRINTED IN THE UNITED STATES OF AMERICA

———𝓋𝓋𝓋———

To my beloved bride Dawn:
"Ti amo, Alba, sempre."

Contents

—·⚬∾∾⚬·—

Introduction

The word "papacy" comes from the Italian word *papa* (or "pope") which means "father." It describes the Catholic Church's supreme teaching office, established by Jesus Christ for Peter and his successors. Christ instituted this divine office in the Church to ensure the continuity and integrity of His Gospel message throughout the ages, and to provide a perpetual and visible source of unity for the Christian family until His Second Coming. The pope is our spiritual papa, or father, and the Vicar of Jesus Christ on earth.

Unlike Protestants, who view their pastors or even themselves as the final arbiter of God's Word, Catholics recognize that this is the exalted task of the pope and the bishops in communion with him. As we will see in the Scriptures, the pope speaks for Christ on matters of the Christian faith, and he rules and governs the One, Holy, Catholic and Apostolic Church.[1] Having one man in charge prevents divisions and chaos, which afflict the more than thirty thousand different Protestant Christian denominations today.

The papacy is the longest-living institution in the civilized world. During the last twenty centuries, 264 men have succeeded to Peter's position to head the Catholic Church. The papacy has survived for almost two thousand years. Under the authority of her popes, the Catholic Church has defined the major tenets of the Christian faith that are accepted by Catholics and Protestants

---

[1] The word "Catholic" comes from the Greek word *katholikos*, which means "according to the whole," or more commonly, "universal." The word has been used to describe the Church since apostolic times.

alike. These include the fundamental doctrines of the Trinity, Christology, and the canon of Scripture that we will discuss later.

The Bible reveals Peter's unique position among the rest of the apostles. For example, Jesus tells Peter alone: "Thou art Peter; and upon this rock I will build my church, and the gates of hell shall not prevail against it" (Mt 16:18). Jesus places Peter in charge of the Church and promises to protect his teachings from error: "I will give to thee the keys of the kingdom of heaven. And whatsoever thou shalt bind upon earth, it shall be bound also in heaven: and whatsoever thou shalt loose on earth, it shall be loosed also in heaven" (Mt 16:19). Jesus also tells Peter to strengthen the other apostles (see Lk 22:32), and appoints Peter the chief shepherd of the Church when He tells him: "Feed my lambs. . . . Tend my sheep. . . . Feed my sheep . . ." (Jn 21:15-17).[2]

This book will examine these and many other Scripture verses that support the Catholic Church's teaching on the papacy. In explaining the Catholic position, we will quote exclusively from Scripture in all but the last chapter on the early Church Fathers. We will also use the technique of biblical interpretation viewed by Protestants as essential to understanding God's Word: *Scriptura sui ipsius interpres*. This is Latin for "Scripture alone interprets itself."

This technique focuses on using Old Testament revelations to explain the revelations in the New Testament. It is soundly based on the truth that God's revelation builds upon itself, and that biblical truths of the present are often explained only by understanding the revelations that have preceded them. As Augustine said: "The New Testament is concealed in the Old, and the Old is revealed in the New." When we employ this maxim, we unlock the biblical meaning of terms such as the "keys," "kingdom of heaven," "gates of hell," "binding and loosing," and many other concepts relating to Peter and his supreme role in the Church.

---

[2] RSV-CE.

In discussing the papacy, non-Catholics often have the impression that Catholics exalt the pope and the Church over the Scriptures. Nothing could be further from the truth. Catholics believe that the Scriptures are the inspired and infallible Word of God, dictated to the sacred writers by the Holy Spirit, and thus inerrant on all that they teach.[3] Sadly, many Protestant communities, which base their faith on the Bible alone, have abandoned this traditional understanding of Scripture.

Catholics and many other Christians recognize the historical fact that we have received the Scriptures *through the Catholic Church*. The Catholic Church existed before the New Testament Scriptures. Her earliest members wrote the Scriptures. She transmitted the Scriptures from the original autographs that are no longer extant. She preserved and protected the Scriptures in the face of bloody persecutions. She determined the canon of Scripture. She handed the Scriptures down through the ages. The Church, under the successive leadership of her popes, has been the custodian of Sacred Scripture throughout Christian history. Indeed, the Church is the servant of Scripture. Those who believe in the inspiration of the Bible owe a tremendous debt to the Catholic Church.

This is why Paul calls the Church "the pillar and ground of the truth" (1 Tim 3:15). Paul describes the Church this way because she has received and is the caretaker of the Word of God, which is the whole of God's self-revelation consummated in Jesus Christ. This Word includes not only Scripture (the written dimension) but the oral apostolic Tradition (the unwritten dimension) as well. Paul tells us to "stand fast; and hold the traditions which you

---

[3] See, for example, Second Vatican Council, the Dogmatic Constitution on Divine Revelation (*Dei Verbum*), No. 11; Pius XII, *Divino Afflante Spiritu* (1943); Benedict XV, *Spiritus Paraclitus* (1920); Pius X, *Lamentabili Sane* (1907); Leo XIII, *Providentissimus Deus* (1893); and Pius IX, *Syllabus of Errors* (1864).

have learned, whether by word, or by our epistle" (2 Thess 2:14). While Protestants generally exalt the written Tradition (the Bible) over all else, Scripture does no such thing. Instead, Scripture requires us to follow *both* the written *and unwritten* Tradition.

Thus, when Catholics talk about the Bible, we want to make sure that all Christians understand its proper place in the economy of God's revelation. The Bible is the written Word of God for sure, but it is only one of the two components that make up the single Deposit of Faith that Christ gave to His apostles, as Scripture itself teaches. This Deposit of Faith has been entrusted by God to the Catholic Church, under the guidance of the Holy Spirit and protection of the successors of Peter.

Catholics also want to ensure that Scripture is properly interpreted with the mind of the Church. After all, the Spirit who gave the Church the Bible is the same Spirit who guides the Church's interpretation of the Bible. When Christians attempt to interpret the Scriptures outside of the living tradition and teaching authority of the Catholic Church, Peter says: "The unlearned and unstable wrest [them], as they do also the other scriptures, to their own destruction" (2 Pet 3:16).

Since this book is about the papacy, we will quote from the Douay-Rheims Bible, which is a word-for-word translation of the Latin Vulgate.[4] Jerome, under Pope Damasus (the thirty-sixth successor to Peter), translated the original Hebrew and Greek texts into the Latin Vulgate at the end of the fourth century. The Latin Vulgate is the oldest and most accurate translation of Scripture, and the official translation of the Catholic Church.

---

[4] In a number of places, the *Catholic Edition of the Revised Standard Version* (RSV-CE) will be used. With the exception of book titles that are unique to the Douay-Rheims version, abbreviations are those used in the RSV-CE.

The Latin Vulgate was translated into English by Catholic scholars at Rheims in 1582 (New Testament) and Douay in 1609 (Old Testament). The Douay-Rheims Bible was revised and diligently compared with the Latin Vulgate by Bishop Richard Challoner in 1749-1752. The text used in this book is taken from the Douay-Rheims 1899 edition of the John Murphy Company, Baltimore, Maryland, by TAN Books in 1971. The earliest Protestant Bible translation, the King James Version, was largely based on the Douay-Rheims Bible.[5]

I have written this book for both Catholics and non-Catholics who want a better understanding of the biblical basis for the papacy. This book provides an introduction to the basic doctrines of papal authority, infallibility, and apostolic succession. The book also addresses the most common misconceptions about the papacy, and answers the most frequent rebuttals of Catholic teaching about the papacy. Further study, particularly of the early Church Fathers, is encouraged and recommended.

When this book is read with an open mind, I trust that the reader will see the explicit biblical precedents for the papacy. I also pray that all Christians come to recognize God's incredible gift in the papacy. This office, first held by Peter, has been the visible source of unity for the Christian family for the past twenty centuries. It is only through our union with Peter that we "may be made perfect in one," as our Lord so strongly desires (Jn 17:23).

---

[5] The first translation of the King James Version came out in 1611 and included the deuterocanonical books, which non-Catholics erroneously call the "Apocrypha." They are: Tobias (Tobit in RSV-CE), Judith, Wisdom, Ecclesiasticus (Sirach), Baruch, and 1 and 2 Machabees (Maccabees); there are also parts of Daniel (3:24-90; 13:7-14, 42) and Esther (10:4-16, 24). The deuterocanonical books have always been part of the Catholic canon. They were also included in the Septuagint, from which Jesus and the apostles quote throughout the New Testament. Today, most Protestant Bibles do not include the deuterocanonical books.

If someone does not hold fast to this unity of Peter, can he imagine that he still holds the faith? If he desert the chair of Peter upon whom the Church was built, can he still be confident that he is in the Church?

— Cyprian, c. A.D. 246

JOHN SALZA
The Ascension of the Lord
May 25, Anno Domini 2006

—⟨⟩⟨⟩⟨⟩—

CHAPTER ONE

Peter Is 'The First' Among the Apostles

The scriptural support for Peter's preeminence in the early Church and the special role that Jesus gave Peter is clear and convincing. Peter is mentioned no less than 195 times in the New Testament, while the other apostles combined are mentioned less frequently. The Apostle John, the disciple whom Jesus loved and who had a profound theological influence on the early Church, is mentioned less than 30 times (the next most mentioned apostle). In the first 15 chapters of the book of Acts, which recounts the first 15 years of the infant Church, Peter is mentioned 56 times. Peter is clearly the leader of the early Church.

Further, with only two exceptions addressed below, Peter is always mentioned first when named among the other apostles.[1] Judas Iscariot, the apostle who betrayed Jesus, is always mentioned last. This polarity between Peter and Judas Iscariot is not mere coincidence — Peter was the leader and Judas was the traitor. We see this ordering in Matthew 10:2-4:

> And the names of the twelve apostles are these: *The first*, Simon who is called Peter, and Andrew his brother, James the son of Zebedee, and John his brother, Philip and Bartholomew, Thomas and Matthew the publican, and

---

[1] See, for example, Mk 16:7; Acts 1:15; 2:14, 37; 8:14; 10:45; 1 Cor 9:5; 15:5.

James the son of Alpheus, and Thaddeus, Simon the Cananean, and Judas Iscariot, who also betrayed him.[2]

The description of Simon as "the first" (in Greek, *protos*) is a special title that means "first and foremost" or "primary first." Peter's description as "the first" is not an arbitrary numerical detail or a chronological indicator of when Peter became an apostle. In fact, Peter was not the first apostle to follow Jesus. In John's Gospel, we learn that Andrew, Peter's brother, was the first apostle to have faith in Jesus as the Messiah (see Jn 1:41) and introduced Peter to Jesus (see Jn 1:42). Yet, Matthew gives Peter the title "primary one," or *protos*. When Jesus met Simon (Peter), He immediately changed his name to Cephas, which is Aramaic for "rock"[3] (much more on this later).

Matthew uses the same word *protos* as he records Jesus' description of the chief leader, or "the first" of His kingdom (Mt 20:27).[4] In contrasting His kingdom with that of the Gentiles, Jesus says that the princes of the Gentiles lord their authority over their subjects (see v. 25), and says that it must not be so among His apostles (see v. 26). Jesus then says that "he that will be first [*protos*] among you, shall be your servant. Even as the Son of man is not come to be ministered unto, but to minister, and to give his life a redemption for many" (vv. 27-28).

Jesus contrasts the authority of His "first" with the authority of the Gentiles, which demonstrates that *protos* describes one who is in authority. Jesus further connects "the first" with "authority" by comparing "the first" to "even . . . the Son of man" (v. 28). In

---

[2] See also Lk 6:13-16; Acts 1:13. Unless otherwise noted, italicized text in Scripture quotes has been emphasized by the author.

[3] See Jn 1:42; see also Mk 3:16.

[4] Since tradition holds that Peter provided Mark the information for his Gospel and would not have boasted about his lofty position, it is not surprising to see that Mark does not use *protos* to describe Peter.

this way, Jesus explains that the first in authority must really be the first in service. Jesus, who is the Supreme authority, became the Supreme servant by laying His life down in sacrifice. Jesus teaches that "the first" of His kingdom must do likewise. This shows that *protos* designates a rank of preeminence, not a mere numerical rank, and is defined by self-sacrificing leadership. Peter, "the first" of Jesus' kingdom, followed His Master's example by also laying his life down in sacrifice.[5]

Other New Testament writers use *protos* to describe the pre-eminent person or thing among a group of its kind. For example, in the parable of the prodigal son, Luke writes: "And the father said to his servants: Bring forth quickly *the first robe*, and put it on him, and put a ring on his hand, and shoes on his feet" (Lk 15:22). The *first* robe was the *best* of all the robes that the father could give his son. Luke also uses *protos* to describe "the *chief man* of the island, named Publius" (Acts 28:7). Publius was the chief magistrate of the island of Melita, a man with authority. Paul also humbly describes himself as a sinner, "of whom I am *the chief*" (1 Tim 1:15). *Protos* means the chief or first among persons or things of its kind.

We also see *protos* being used as a title of preeminence in the Septuagint translation of the Old Testament. For example, in the second book of Esdras (also known as Nehemiah), the sacred writer describes the "*chief singers* appointed, to praise with canticles, and give thanks to God."[6] We also see *protos* describe "Azarias *the high priest*, and all the rest of the priests."[7] Again, *protos* describes the chief or preeminent person in a group of people (singers, priests, etc.). Peter is described as "the first" (Mt 10:2) among the apostles because he is the chief apostle and leader of the apostolic Church.

---

[5] See Jn 13:36; 21:18; 2 Pet 1:14.

[6] 2 Esd 12:45 (2 Neh in RSV-CE).

[7] 2 Para 26:20 (2 Chron in RSV-CE).

The Two Exceptions

As we mentioned, there are only two instances where Peter is not mentioned first among the apostles. These two instances are conspicuous exceptions to the scriptural rule. The first is found in 1 Corinthians 3:22, where Paul writes: "For all things are yours, whether it be Paul, or Apollo, or Cephas, or the world, or life, or death, or things present, or things to come; for all are yours."

While it appears that Paul puts Peter (Cephas) last in this grouping, Paul is actually listing these names in the order of ascending authority. We see this in the very next verse where Paul's order ascends from Peter to Christ to God: "And you are Christ's; and Christ is God's" (v. 23). Paul uses a similar ordering between woman, man, Christ and God later in the same letter: "But I would have you know, that the head of every man is Christ; and the head of the woman is the man; and the head of Christ is God" (1 Cor 11:3).[8] We also see Paul's use of ascending importance earlier in the same letter to the Corinthians when he writes: "Now this I say, that every one of you saith: I indeed am of Paul; and I am of Apollo; and I am of Cephas; and I of Christ" (1 Cor 1:12).[9]

Paul's order ascends from Paul (the least) to Christ (the greatest). This means that Peter is still "the first" among the apostles, and that Paul, in his humility, places himself last. Paul provides a similar order later in the same letter when he writes: "Have we not power to carry about a woman, a sister, as well as the rest of the apostles, and the brethren of the Lord, and Cephas?" (1 Cor 9:5). Once again, Paul's order of importance ascends from religious

---

[8] While the Church teaches that men and women have equal dignity, the Church also teaches that wives must be submissive to their husbands in all things lawful, which reflects the order of creation. See, for example, Eph 5:22-24; Col 3:18; Tit 2:5; and 1 Pet 3:1-2.

[9] Because Paul employs this literary technique (ascending authority) in the same letter (1 Cor 1:12 and 3:22), we have counted these two occurrences as *one* exception to the general rule. The other exception is in Gal 2:9.

women, to the apostles, to the brethren of the Lord (probably James, Joseph, Simon and Judas),[10] to Peter. The fact that Paul invariably distinguishes Peter from the rest of the apostles, whether in ascending or descending importance, underscores Peter's primacy among them.

The second instance where Peter is not listed first among the apostles is in Galatians 2:9: "And when they had known the grace that was given to me, James and Cephas and John, who seemed to be pillars, gave to me and Barnabas the right hands of fellowship: that we should go unto the Gentiles, and they unto the circumcision." This is the *only* instance in the New Testament in which Peter (Cephas) is listed in the midst of other apostles (and not first or last).

Since it is the only instance, it can hardly be used to diminish Peter's preeminence that pervades the rest of Scripture. In fact, this order seemed so unnatural to many of the early Church fathers, they actually rewrote the order as Peter, James and John in many of their writings! (This can be seen in the writings of Marcion, Irenaeus, Tertullian, Origen, Gregory of Nyssa, Jerome, Ambrose, Ephraem, and Augustine.)

Nevertheless, there seems to be a plausible explanation for this glowing exception. Paul was writing to the Galatians who were Gentile Christians. As Gentiles, the Galatians were never under the Mosaic law of circumcision. Paul's principal mission, as the apostle to the Gentiles, was to explain to them that circumcision was no longer necessary in God's New Covenant.

Paul highlights this in the two verses preceding Galatians 2:9, where he distinguishes his role of evangelizing the uncircumcised Gentiles from that of Peter, who had a peculiar charge to evangelize the Jews. Paul writes: "But contrariwise, when they had seen that to me was committed the gospel of the uncircumcision,

---

[10] See Mt 13:55 and Mk 6:3.

as to Peter was that of the circumcision. (For he who wrought in Peter to the apostleship of the circumcision, wrought in me also among the Gentiles)" (vv. 7-8).

After Paul explains his God-given role to the Gentiles, he describes *when* the Gentiles came to know the grace that was given to him, James, Peter, and John (see v. 9). Thus, the order of "Paul, James, Peter, and John" simply describes the order from whom the Gentiles learned of their inclusion in the New Covenant. They would have most likely heard this good news from Paul first (who had a specific mission to the Gentiles) and only later from Peter (who had a general commission over the Church and a specific duty to the Jews). Thus, this unique ordering of Paul, James, Peter, and John has nothing to do with their apostolic importance.

Other Examples of Peter's Primacy

We see Peter's formation as the leader of the apostles during Jesus' earthly ministry, particularly when Peter speaks on behalf of the apostles. Here are some examples:

- Peter is the first to confess the divinity of Jesus Christ: "Thou art Christ, the Son of the living God."[11]
- Peter is the only apostle to speak at the Transfiguration: "Master, it is good for us to be here; and let us make three tabernacles, one for thee, and one for Moses, and one for Elias; not knowing what he said" (Lk 9:33).
- Peter is the only apostle to discern the meaning of the washing of feet: "Lord, dost thou wash my feet? . . . Thou shalt never wash my feet. . . . Lord, not only my feet, but also my hands and my head."[12]

---

[11] Mt 16:16; see also Mk 8:29; Jn 6:70.
[12] Jn 13:6, 8-9.

- Peter discerns the rule of forgiveness on behalf of the apostles: "Lord, how often shall my brother offend against me, and I forgive him? till seven times?" (Mt 18:21).
- Peter discerns the parable of the householder on behalf of the apostles: "Lord, dost thou speak this parable to us, or likewise to all?" (Lk 12:41).
- Peter is the only apostle to articulate the effects of Jesus' curse on the fig tree: "Rabbi, behold the fig tree, which thou didst curse, is withered away" (Mk 11:21).
- Peter declares on behalf of the apostles that they have left everything to follow Jesus: "Behold we have left all things, and have followed thee: what therefore shall we have?"[13]
- Peter answers Jesus' question about who touched His garment on behalf of the apostles: "Master, the multitudes throng and press thee, and dost thou say, Who touched me?" (Lk 8:45).
- Peter alone asks Jesus if he can walk to Him on the water, and Jesus empowers Peter to do so: "Lord, if it be thou, bid me come to thee upon the waters. And he said: Come. And Peter going down out of the boat, walked upon the water to come to Jesus."[14]
- Peter alone plunges himself into the sea and runs toward Jesus after the miraculous catch of fish: "Simon Peter, when he heard that it was the Lord, girt his coat about him, (for he was naked,) and cast himself into the sea."[15] Also, only Peter is described as hauling the net of fish to shore: "Simon Peter went up, and drew the net to land, full of great fishes, one hundred and fifty-three."[16]

---

[13] Mt 19:27; Mk 10:28.
[14] Mt 14:28-29.
[15] Jn 21:7.
[16] Jn 21:11.

Peter is also distinguished from the other apostles in a variety of ways. For example:

- An angel identifies Peter as the leader of the apostles as he confirms to Mary Magdalene and Mary the mother of James the resurrection of Jesus: "But go, tell his disciples and Peter that he goeth before you into Galilee; there you shall see him, as he told you" (Mk 16:7).

- The Gospel writers reveal a seemingly insignificant detail about how John arrived at Christ's empty tomb first, but waited to let Peter enter before him: "And they both ran together, and that other disciple did outrun Peter, and came first to the sepulchre. And when he stooped down, he saw the linen cloths lying; but yet he went not in. Then cometh Simon Peter, following him, and went into the sepulchre."[17]

- The two disciples of Emmaus specify how Peter saw the risen Lord, even though they had just seen Jesus the previous hour: "And rising up, the same hour, they went back to Jerusalem: and they found the eleven gathered together, and those that were staying with them, saying: The Lord is risen indeed, and hath appeared to Simon."[18]

- Paul also distinguishes between Jesus' post-resurrection appearances to Peter and everyone else: "And that he was buried, and that he rose again the third day, according to the scriptures: And that he was seen by Cephas; and after that by the eleven. Then he was seen by more than five hundred brethren at once."[19]

---

[17] Jn 20:4-6; see also Lk 24:12.
[18] Lk 24:33-34.
[19] 1 Cor 15:4-6.

Jesus also singles out Peter from the rest of the apostles. For example:

- Outsiders approach Peter for Jesus' temple tax (the didrachma), treating Peter as the Vicar and spokesman for Jesus: "Doth not your master pay the didrachmas?"[20] Jesus responds with a miracle, paying the tax for both Himself and Peter, telling him to "go to the sea, and cast in a hook: and that fish which shall first come up, take: and when thou hast opened its mouth, thou shalt find a stater: take that, and give it to them for me and thee."[21]
- Jesus chooses Peter's ship from which to teach the crowds: "And going into one of the ships that was Simon's, he desired him to draw back a little from the land. And sitting he taught the multitudes out of the ship" (Lk 5:3). Peter's boat is a metaphor for the Church, which is often called the "barque of Peter."
- Jesus tells Peter alone to cast his net for fish, and a miraculous catch follows: "Now when he had ceased to speak, he said to Simon: Launch out into the deep, and let down your nets for a draught" (Lk 5:4). Peter leads the evangelism of the Church, for Jesus says to Peter alone: "Fear not: from henceforth thou shalt catch men" (Lk 5:10).

Jesus further distinguishes Peter from the rest of the apostles by appointing him as the leader or "father" (papa or pope) of the Church. As we will see, Jesus appoints Peter alone as the rock of the Church and the keeper of the keys to the kingdom of heaven. Jesus gives Peter the divine authority to bind and loose, and charges Peter alone to feed and rule over the Church. Jesus also prays that Peter's faith may not fail and commands Peter to

---

[20] Mt 17:23.
[21] Mt 17:26.

strengthen the other apostles. After Christ's ascension into heaven, Peter leads the early Church by his authoritative teachings and no one questions him.

These and many other biblical events demonstrate that Jesus intended to leave us a visible Church with *one man in charge*. That man is Peter, and his successors throughout the ages, which Scripture, Tradition, and history affirm. Let us now examine these events in detail by "searching the Scriptures."[22]

---

[22] See Jn 5:39.

CHAPTER TWO

Peter Is the Rock of the Church

Peter's unique role as "the first" of the apostles is definitively set forth in Matthew 16:13-19. This is one of the most important texts that establish the biblical basis for the papacy.

Jesus sets the stage by taking His apostles into Caesarea Philippi, which was a district built by Herod's son Philip as a dedication to Caesar.

The area was almost 1,200 feet above sea level and housed a massive rock formation about 200 feet high and 500 hundred feet wide at the base of Mount Hermon. There was a large, deep cavern in the rock formation, from which the springs of the river Jordan flowed. At the top of the rock formation was a temple dedicated to Caesar, and at the bottom a sanctuary dedicated to Pan, the pagan god of shepherds and flocks.

Jesus, the true God of shepherds and flocks, deliberately chose this metaphorical backdrop to rename Simon "rock" (Peter, or *Petros* in Greek, comes from the Greek word *petra*, which means "rock"). In this setting, Jesus announced that He would build His divine kingdom in opposition to the worldly kingdom of Caesar, and confer upon Peter the office of chief shepherd of the Church. Let's examine this passage in some detail.

> And Jesus came into the quarters of Cesarea Philippi: and he asked his disciples, saying: Whom do men say that the Son of man is? But they said: Some John the Baptist, and other some Elias, and others Jeremias, or one of the prophets. Jesus saith to them: But whom do you say that I

am? Simon Peter answered and said: Thou art Christ, the Son of the living God. And Jesus answering, said to him: Blessed art thou, Simon Bar-Jona: because flesh and blood hath not revealed it to thee, but my Father who is in heaven. And I say to thee: That thou art Peter; and upon this rock I will build my church, and the gates of hell shall not prevail against it. And I will give to thee the keys of the kingdom of heaven. And whatsoever thou shalt bind upon earth, it shall be bound also in heaven: and whatsoever thou shalt loose upon earth, it shall be loosed also in heaven.[1]

Perhaps more ink has been spilled about this passage than any other when discussing the biblical basis for the papacy. There are many critical things happening in this all-important passage. We will tackle them one at a time.

After Jesus asks His disciples who He is, Simon alone responds by declaring: "Thou art Christ, the Son of the living God" (v. 16). We thus see something incredibly unique. God the Father gives Simon a divine revelation about Jesus, which Simon then verbally communicates to Jesus and the other apostles. No other apostle had been given the gift. God initiates the heavenly decree by penetrating the mind of Simon, and moving him to make the infallible declaration. Jesus confirms the heavenly origin of Simon's decree by saying: "Blessed art thou, Simon Bar-Jona: because flesh and blood hath not *revealed* it to thee, *but my Father who is in heaven*" (v. 17).

We will address the biblical basis for Simon Peter's ability to teach infallibly in more depth as we proceed. But, at this point, we note that Simon's ability to receive divine theological insights from God (here, a Christological truth) and communicate them without error forms the basis for the Catholic understanding of papal infallibility.

---

[1] Mt 16:13-19.

Simon Peter's ability to communicate infallibly has nothing to do with his faith per se, for the other apostles also had faith in Jesus. In fact, Matthew 16:13-19 says nothing about Simon's faith at all. Simon does not say: "I believe thou art Christ." Simon says: "Thou art Christ." Jesus responds by blessing Simon, not for his faith, but for communicating the revelation he received from the heavenly Father.

Simon Peter's infallibility also has nothing to do with his intellect or education. Scripture even describes Peter as "illiterate and ignorant" (Acts 4:13). Such a description means that Peter had no formal training in theology. This underscores God's divine intervention into the mind of Simon Peter, a man without any theological training, and yet the only apostle to confess a profound, theological truth about Jesus Christ.

God chose the uneducated Simon to emphasize that He (and not Simon) would really be the one in charge of guiding His Church into the truth, as Jesus later promises the other apostles.[2] As Paul says: "But the foolish things of the world hath God chosen, that he may confound the wise; and the weak things of the world hath God chosen, that he may confound the strong" (1 Cor 1:27).

In response to Simon's revelatory declaration, Jesus declares to him: "And I say to thee: That thou art Peter; and upon this rock I will build my church, and the gates of hell shall not prevail against it" (v. 18). This is another extremely significant verse. We see that, after Simon makes his infallible decree about Jesus, Jesus changes Simon's name to Peter (in Greek, *Petros*), which means "rock." As we saw in John 1:42, Matthew records Simon's new name as "Cephas" (also spelled *Kepha*), which is a Greek transliteration of the Aramaic word "rock."[3] Now, in Matthew 16:13-19, we find out *why* Jesus changed Simon's name (to Cephas, Kepha, Petros, Peter, rock).

---

[2] See Jn 14:16, 26; 16:13.
[3] See also 1 Cor 1:12; 3:22; 9:5; 15:5 and Gal 2:9.

In Jewish tradition, names were very important and functioned principally as titles that defined a person's role in society. In fact, in the Jewish Torah, changing a person's name meant changing the person's spiritual status and mission. We see this throughout Scripture. For example, when God established His covenant with Abram, God changed his name from Abram (in Hebrew, meaning "father") to Abraham (meaning "father of nations" or "chief of the multitude"): "Neither shall thy name be called any more Abram: but thou shalt be called Abraham: because I have made thee a father of many nations" (Gen 17:5). By changing his name, God changed Abraham's mission from a chieftain of a family tribe to the spiritual father of the Jewish nation.

God did the same thing with Jacob, Abraham's grandson. When God appointed Jacob to be the founder of the twelve tribes of Israel, he changed Jacob's name to Israel, which in Hebrew means "who prevails with God": "But he said: Thy name shall not be called Jacob, but Israel: for if thou hast been strong against God, how much more shalt thou prevail against men?" (Gen 32:28). Thus, God chose Abraham and Israel to be the earthly shepherds of His covenant with the Jews, and designated their new roles by changing their name, and hence, their spiritual mission.

Jesus changed Simon's name to *Petros* to designate his new spiritual role among the apostles, and the Jews would have immediately understood its significance. This reflected the spiritual insight that Simon received from God the Father. Simon was now called "rock," which designated him as the foundation upon which Jesus would build His Church. Peter's unique role is highlighted by the fact that "rock" was not a proper name in Jesus' time. Archeological and historical evidence demonstrate that Simon was the first man who ever had the name "Peter." And like the roles of Abraham and Israel, who served as earthly shepherds of God's people in the Old Testament, Simon Peter would be the earthly shepherd of God's people in the New and Everlasting Testament.

There is a clear exchange of titles between Simon Peter and Jesus. Simon calls Jesus "the Christ," and Jesus calls Simon "the rock." Since Simon's confession was elicited by Jesus' question — "But who do you say that I am?" — Jesus is now telling Simon *who he is as well.* Jesus' declaration is responsive to and parallels Simon's declaration. In other words, since Simon revealed the true character and identity of Jesus (the Messiah and Son of God), Jesus revealed the true character and identity of Simon Peter (the stable, sturdy, infallible foundation of the Church). This exchange perhaps comes out more forcefully in the Greek language: Jesus, you are the *Christos!* Simon, you are the *Petros!*

Because this verse is compelling proof that Christ intended to build a visible Church upon the person of Peter, non-Catholics have offered several rebuttals to the Catholic position. Before we address the significance of Peter's "keys of the kingdom of heaven" (v. 19) and his authority to "bind and loose" (v. 19), we will address the most common arguments against Simon Peter's designation as the rock foundation of Christ's Church.

The "Jesus Builds the Church on Peter's Faith" Argument

One of the most common arguments that non-Catholics advance is that Jesus in Matthew 16:18 is building His Church upon Peter's *faith*, and not Peter himself. While Peter is visible, Peter's faith is invisible. Thus, if Jesus is building His Church upon the invisible faith of Peter, then the Church must also be an invisible association. Since the Catholic Church is a visible institution (marked by a pope, bishops, priests, and deacons) that claims visible authority, the non-Catholic argues that it cannot be Christ's true Church.

This argument fails to pass biblical muster for several reasons. First and most obviously, Jesus does not say that He is going to build

His Church upon Peter's faith. In fact, Matthew 16:13-19 says nothing about Peter's faith at all. As we saw above, when Simon Peter declares that Jesus is the Christ, Jesus affirms that Peter is declaring a *revelation* from the Father, *not* making a statement of personal faith. While Peter certainly had faith in Jesus, the revelation that he received and communicated existed independently of his faith.

God does not base one's ability to teach infallibly upon his faith. The high priest Caiphas is biblical proof of this truth. Caiphas had no faith in Jesus Christ. In fact, he rejected Jesus' claims and plotted His death. Nevertheless, God used Caiphas to issue the infallible prophecy about Christ's death on the cross, which we read in the Gospel of John: "Now Caiphas was he who had given the counsel to the Jews: That it was expedient that one man should die for the people" (Jn 18:14).

Jesus also wanted the apostles to understand the distinction between personal faith and the ability to communicate God's infallible word, which Peter would have the ongoing ability to do. This is why, immediately after Peter's infallible declaration, Jesus explained to them that the basis for Peter's communication was a heavenly revelation from the Father, not a statement of personal faith by Peter. Jesus did this to emphasize that the office He was now creating would be based upon God's divine protection and intervention, and not the officeholder's personal faith.

Jesus followed His affirmation by giving Simon a new title, in response to the title that Simon gave Jesus. Since Simon Peter declared a truth about the *person* of Jesus (calling him the "Christ"), Jesus declared a truth about the *person* of Simon Peter (calling him the "rock"). Therefore, when Jesus said that He would build His Church "upon this rock" (v. 18), He was referring to the *person* of Peter, not his faith (which was only one aspect of Peter's person).

Jesus' designation of the person of Peter as the rock foundation of His Church is further demonstrated by the inspired Greek text. Jesus said He would build His Church "upon *this* rock" (in

Greek, *epi tautee tee petra*). Jesus did not say "upon *the* rock" (*epi tee petra*) or "upon *a* rock" (*epi petra*). The Greek word *tautee* is a demonstrative adjective that means "this." The use of the demonstrative adjective requires a referent to complete the connection between it and what it is describing.

The text is clear that this referent is "rock" (*petra*), which is another word for Peter (*Petros*). (As we will further address below, Matthew calls Simon *Petros* instead of *petra* to reflect the masculine nature of Peter, since *petra* is a feminine noun.) If Christ said that He would build His Church "upon the rock" or "upon a rock" instead of "upon this rock," the referent would have been less clear and could have conceivably been pointing to someone or something other than Peter. But since Jesus said "upon *this* rock," the referent can only be Peter. Moreover, since Peter's faith is never mentioned in the passage, faith could not have been the referent even if Jesus had used one of the alternative phrases "upon the rock" or "upon a rock."

The grammatical rule becomes even clearer if we make *tautee* a demonstrative pronoun — that is, without an accompanying noun. For example, if Jesus had said: "You are Peter, and upon *this* I will build my Church," the demonstrative pronoun (*tautee*) would relate back to the nearest referent, which is Peter. If we replace the demonstrative pronoun with a definite or indefinite article, it is no longer obvious that the referent is Peter: "You are Peter, and upon *the* I will build my Church" or "You are Peter, and upon *a* I will build my Church."

The demonstrative force of *tautee* is so strong that elsewhere in Scripture it is translated as "this same." For example:

- In 1 Corinthians 7:20, Paul says: "Let every man abide in *the same* [*tautee*] calling in which he was called."
- In 2 Corinthians 8:6, Paul says: "Insomuch, that we desired Titus, that as he had begun, so also he would finish among you *this same* [*tautee*] grace."

- In Acts 13:33, Paul also says: "*This same* [*tautee*] God hath fulfilled to our children, raising up Jesus."

The King James Version of the Bible translates *tautee* "this same" way. If we were to apply this force to the demonstrative adjective in Matthew 16:18, the verse would read: "Thou art Peter; and upon this *same* rock I will build my church."

That Jesus turns the whole dialogue upon the *person* of Peter after Peter confesses the Father's revelation further demonstrates that Jesus is not building the Church upon Peter's faith, but Peter himself. Jesus says: "Blessed are *you*, Simon, for flesh and blood has not revealed it to *you*. And I say to *you*, *you* are Peter, and upon this rock I will build my Church. I will give *you* the keys of the kingdom, and whatever *you* bind or loose on earth will be bound or loosed in heaven." The word "you," from the Greek *soi*, is singular and therefore refers to the *person* of Peter.

We also note that Jesus says: "Thou art Peter; *and* upon this rock I will build my church" (Matthew 16:18). The word "and" (in Greek, *kai*) further intensifies the connection between "Peter" in the first clause and "rock" in the second clause. That is, *kai* serves to join the noun *Petros* with the demonstrative adjective *tautee*. Jesus does not say: "Thou art Peter; *but* upon this rock I will build my church." The word "but" (in Greek, *alla*) would weaken the connection between Peter and rock. If such were used, Peter (*Petros*) would still be a rock, but the conjunctive use of *alla* would suggest that there is another rock (*petra*) upon which Jesus would build His Church. This, of course, is not the case, since Jesus uses "and" to connect *Petros* and *petra*.

Those arguing that Jesus builds His Church upon the faith, and not the person of Peter, also have no biblical precedent for their argument. The Scriptures never equate "rock" with "faith." As we will see below, Scripture always ascribes the word "rock" to *persons*, such as God, Christ, Peter, and Abraham. Further, nowhere does Scripture say that Jesus builds His Church upon "faith," or that "faith" is the foundation or building block of the Church. To the contrary, Scripture says Jesus builds His Church *upon persons*.

For example, Paul says that the Church is:

- "Built upon the *foundation of the apostles and prophets*, Jesus Christ himself being the chief corner stone" (Eph 2:20).
- The Apocalypse (Revelation) also says: "And the wall of the city had *twelve foundations*, and in them, the twelve names of the *twelve apostles* of the Lamb" (Rev 21:14).
- Remember also that, in John 1:42, Jesus attributes "rock" (*Cephas*) to Peter's *person*, not his faith or any other attribute of Peter's personhood.

It is interesting to note that Protestants invariably argue that the Church is built upon the "Bible," until they are confronted with Jesus' words in Matthew 16:18, which forces them to argue the Church is built upon the faith of Peter as well. This raises the obvious question: Is the Church built upon the faith of Peter, or the Bible, or both? If it is built upon the Bible, then why doesn't Scripture say that? If it is built upon the faith of Peter, then why does Paul say it is built upon all of the apostles who wrote the New Testament, as well as the prophets who wrote the Old (see Eph 2:20)?

Paul also says that the Church (in Greek, *ecclesia*) is the "pillar and ground of the truth."[4] Elsewhere in Scripture, Paul calls the apostles "pillars,"[5] just as he calls them the "foundation."[6] Again, this means that the Church is built upon "persons," and not "faith" or the "Bible" (specifically, the rock of Peter and the foundation of

---

[4] See 1 Tim 3:15.

[5] See Gal 2:9.

[6] See Eph 2:20.

the other apostles). Paul's teaching also demonstrates that the Church is divine since, even though it is lead by fallible men, it is able to preserve and protect the truth through its pillar and foundation structure.

Jesus also uses the word *ecclesia* to describe His Church, which further demonstrates that Jesus builds His Church upon the person of Peter. The word *ecclesia* refers to a visible, hierarchical institution. Jesus uses the word *ecclesia* only two times in the New Testament, both in reference to His visible Church (see Mt 16:18 and 18:17). Since *ecclesia* invariably refers to a visible organization, it must be built upon a visible foundation as well. If the structure is visible, the foundation must also be visible. Since Peter's faith is invisible, his "faith" cannot be the foundation of the visible *ecclesia*, but his "person" can.

This is demonstrated by the fact that Jesus invests Peter with the authority to "bind and loose" in connection with his status as the rock foundation of the Church (see Mt 16:19). As we will examine in greater detail later on, the words "bind" and "loose" are rabbinical terms that describe Peter's authority to prescribe doctrines, as well as permit or forbid certain actions or things. This would include both inviting and excluding persons from the ecclesial community.

This is also demonstrated in Matthew 18:17-18, where Jesus requires sinners to be brought to the Church for discipline and possible excommunication. Jesus says: "And if he will not hear them: tell the church. And if he will not hear the church, let him be to thee as the heathen and publican." (v. 17). Then Jesus says: "Amen I say to you, whatsoever you shall bind upon earth, shall be bound also in heaven; and whatsoever you shall loose upon earth, shall be loosed also in heaven" (v. 18).

Since "binding" and "loosing" are visible acts of authority with which Christ endowed His Church, this same Church must also be a visible organization, as it is the body that will carry out these visible acts. It is therefore no coincidence that Jesus mentions "binding" and "loosing" only the same two times that He mentions "the Church."[7] The visible Church is the body that will carry out the visible actions of binding and loosing.

This is one reason why Paul uses the word "body" to describe the Church. Specifically, Paul says that the Church is *Christ's body*,[8] of which we are members through baptism. If the Church were really an invisible organization of loosely connected believers in Christ, Paul would have called the Church Christ's "soul," not "body." This is because souls are invisible, and bodies are visible. Bodies also carry out visible actions. Thus, Christ works through His visible body, the Church, built upon Peter, to teach and govern her members. This is more biblical proof that the Church is a *visible entity*, which cannot have an invisible foundation.

The "Rock Is in the Third Person" Argument

Some Protestant apologists argue that Jesus is not referring to Peter as the rock of the second clause "upon this rock" in Matthew 16:18 because Jesus addresses "Peter" in the second person and "rock" in the third person. This is a naïve argument that would appeal only to those without a rudimentary understanding of biblical Greek.

Nouns, such as *petra*, are distinguished by number (here, singular) and gender (here, feminine), but not person. Only pronouns, such as "I," "you," "he," or "she" are distinguished by person. Therefore, it is grammatically incorrect to argue that there is a disconnect between the second-person pronoun "you" (referring to Peter) and the third-person noun "rock" based on person, since person is not a legitimate basis for proving a connection between nouns and pronouns.

---

[7] See Mt 16:18-19; Mt 18:17-18.
[8] See Eph 1:22-23; 5:23, 30-31; Col 1:18, 24.

Even if one argues that nouns are inherently in the third person, this does not mean that first- and second-person pronouns and "third-person" nouns cannot be coupled in the same clause. For example, Jesus links the first-person pronoun "I" with the third-person noun "church" when He says: "I will build my church" (v. 18). Jesus also links the second-person pronoun "you (thee)" with the third-person noun "keys" when He says to Peter: "I will give to thee the keys of the kingdom of heaven" (v. 19).

Obviously, the first- and second-person pronouns ("I" and "you") are connected to the third-person nouns ("church" and "keys") because they are directly acting upon them. The fact that the pronouns are first or second person, and the nouns third person, causes no disjunction between them. In these cases, they are necessarily connected.

To argue that Jesus should have continued to use the second person in addressing Peter (*Petros*) instead of the third person (*petra*) in the phrase "upon this rock" also has no biblical precedent. Jesus had already made it clear that He was addressing Peter by using two personal pronouns: "And I say to *you* [in Greek, *soi*], *you* [in Greek, *su*] are Peter. . . ." It would have been redundant, if not grammatically erroneous, to use a third personal pronoun in the same sentence, which would have read: "And I say to you, you are Peter and upon you the rock."

In fact, there is no place in Scripture where a second person pronoun (such as "you") is placed before a metaphor (like "rock") to clarify the identity of the metaphor. Personal pronouns invariably identify the metaphor that follows. Those making this argument are therefore attempting to impose a rule on Scripture that Scripture itself never uses.

Moreover, highlighting that Jesus switches from the second person "Peter" to the third person "rock" actually emphasizes the truth of the Catholic position — namely, that Jesus is describing not just Peter, *but his perpetual office*, when referring to the "rock." The office of Peter would necessarily be described in the third person, as Jesus does in Matthew 16:18. This is consistent with Jesus' intention to establish the office of Peter as the foundation of the Church.

Thus, Jesus' use of the third person reflects His creation of the Church's supreme teaching office. This office begins with Peter as the rock foundation, and carries on with Peter's successors until the end of time. Since a foundation necessarily requires additional material to complete the intended structure, Peter's office will continue throughout history, as long as Jesus continues to build upon it.

The "God Is Really the Rock" Argument

Non-Catholics will also argue that Peter is not the rock of the Church in Matthew 16:18 because there are many places in the Old Testament where God is called "rock." For example: "The LORD is my rock, and my fortress, my deliverer, my God, my rock, in whom I take refuge."[9] In the New Testament, Jesus Christ, who is God in the flesh, is also called "rock": "And all drank the same spiritual drink; (and they drank of the spiritual rock that followed them, and the rock was Christ)" (1 Cor 10:4). If Scripture calls God and Jesus "rock," the non-Catholic argues that Peter cannot also be the rock.

What these non-Catholics seem to forget is that Jesus renamed Simon "rock" in John 1:42: "And Jesus looking upon him, said: Thou art Simon the son of Jona: thou shalt be called Cephas, which is interpreted Peter."[10] As we mentioned, "Cephas" is the Greek transliteration of the Aramaic word for "rock." Non-Catholics generally do not dispute this fact. Therefore, we don't need Matthew 16:18 to prove that Simon Peter is the "rock," since Jesus gave him that title in John 1:42.

---

[9] 2 Sam 22:2-3 (RSV-CE). See also 2 Sam 22:32, 47; 23:3; Ps 18:2, 31, 46; 19:14; 28:1; 42:9; 62:2, 6-7; 89:26; 94:22; 144:1-2 (RSV-CE).

[10] See also Mk 3:16.

Since it is indisputable that Jesus renamed Simon "rock" in John 1:42, it defies reason to argue that Jesus was not referring to Simon as the "rock" in Matthew 16:18. In fact, Jesus called Simon the "son of Jona" in both Matthew 16:17 and John 1:42, the same time that Jesus renamed Simon "rock." This is further proof of the connection between these Gospel verses: Simon is the "son of Jona" and "rock" in both verses.

The argument that "only God is the rock" also assumes that attributions used in Scripture apply only to one person. This is not true. For example:

- In Ephesians 2:20, the apostles are called the foundation of the Church.
- In 1 Corinthians 3:11, Jesus is called the foundation of the Church.

- In 1 Corinthians 3:12, the faithful build upon the foundation.
- In Matthew 16:18, Jesus builds upon the foundation.

- In 1 Peter 2:5, the faithful are called the stones of God's spiritual house.
- In Acts 4:11, Jesus is called the stone of God's house.

- In 1 Corinthians 3:16, the faithful are the temple of God.
- In Apocalypse 21:22, Jesus is the temple of God.

- In Acts 20:28, the apostles are called the bishops of the flock.
- In 1 Peter 2:25, Jesus is called the bishop of the flock.

If Scripture applies the words "foundation," "builders," "stones," "temple," and "bishop" to both Jesus and His faithful, nothing prevents Scripture from applying the word "rock" to both

Jesus and Peter. Moreover, since Jesus says He is going to build His Church "upon this rock," Jesus cannot, grammatically speaking, be the rock in Matthew 16:18. Instead, Jesus is the builder. Jesus would not be both the builder and the foundation, particularly when He identified Peter as the rock on which He would do the building. As we mentioned, in Jewish society, names identified roles. With the exchange of names in Matthew 16:18 comes a delineation of roles as well. Jesus, the Christ, is the builder of the Church; Peter, the rock, is the core foundation of the Church.

The fact that Scripture applies divine attributes to Peter and the apostles further underscores their heavenly appointments. Even though Peter is the rock of Matthew 16:18, this does not infringe upon the Scripture verses that say "God is the rock" or "Jesus is the rock." The Scriptures repeatedly assign divine attributes to both Jesus and His apostles. We have already seen that Scripture refers to both Jesus and His apostles as "shepherds" and the "foundation." In addition, we see the following:

- In Matthew 16:19, Peter has the keys to the kingdom of heaven (the house of God).
- In Apocalypse 3:7, Jesus has the key of David (the house of God).

- In Matthew 16:19, Peter has the authority to bind and loose (open and shut).
- In Apocalypse 3:7, Jesus has the authority to open and shut (bind and loose).

- In Luke 22:30, the apostles sit upon the heavenly thrones.
- In Apocalypse 7:10, 11, 15, 17, God sits upon His heavenly throne.[11]

---

[11] See also Apoc 3:21 and 4:4 (Rev in RSV-CE), where the saints in heaven sit upon the throne of God; and Apoc 8:3; 12:5; 14:3, 5; 16:17; 19:4-5; 20:11-12; 21:3, 5; 22:1, 3, where God sits upon His throne.

Scripture is clear that Jesus *delegates* His own divine authority to Peter and the apostles. This in no way weakens Jesus' authority. Jesus is the source of all divine authority and He never relinquishes it. It means that Peter and the apostles *derive* their authority from Jesus, just as Jesus receives His authority from the Father. For example, Jesus says:

- "And I dispose to you, as my Father hath disposed to me, a kingdom" (Lk 22:29).
- "All things whatsoever the Father hath, are mine. Therefore I said, that he shall receive of mine, and shew it to you" (Jn 16:15).
- "As thou hast sent me into the world, I also have sent them into the world" (Jn 17:18).
- "As the Father hath sent me, I also send you" (Jn 20:21).

Just as the Father has conferred His authority upon Jesus, Jesus confers His authority upon Peter and the apostles.[12] Thus, Peter can be the "rock" of the Church because Jesus gives Peter the power to be the rock.

Abraham Was the "Rock" of the Old Testament

In addition to John 1:42, Mark 3:16, and Matthew 16:18, where Jesus renames Simon "rock," there is *another* biblical precedent for God calling one of His earthly shepherds a "rock." That person is Abraham. This truth further refutes the non-Catholic argument that only God can be the rock. Isaiah 51:1-2 says:

> Give ear to me, you that follow that which is just, and you that seek the Lord: *look unto* the rock whence you are hewn, and to the hole of the pit from which you are dug

---

[12] See, for example, Jn 5:30; 8:28; 12:49; 14:10 and Mt 28:18, where Jesus explains that what He has, He has received from the Father, which Jesus then gives to His apostles.

out. *Look unto* Abraham your father, and to Sara that bore you: for I called him alone, and blessed him, and multiplied him.

In this passage, God reveals to the nation of Israel that He has established His covenant with them upon the rock of Abraham. The phrase "look unto" connects the rock (in Hebrew, *sur*) in verse 1 with Abraham in verse 2. Thus, the Jewish rabbis professed that their father Abraham was the rock on which God had founded His nation.

The parallels between Abraham and Peter are striking:

- Both were marked with the seal of faith (circumcision, which was first given to Abraham).
- Both were patriarchs of the two major covenants between God and His people.
- Both initially led the implementation of God's covenants with His people (Abraham with circumcision and Peter with baptism).
- Both were vicars of God and shepherds of God's covenant people.
- Both received name changes from God to denote their new status as covenant leaders.
- Both were called "rock" by God.

God has given no other men such important spiritual roles as Peter and Abraham. When Jesus renamed Simon "rock," the Jews would have immediately made the connection between Peter and Abraham. They would have understood that, in Jesus Christ's New Covenant, they were to now "look unto" Peter their father, the chief shepherd and rock of the Church.

The importance of Abraham as the "rock" from whom God's people would be hewn should not be overlooked. The sacred writers emphasize that Abraham is the father of the children of the New

Covenant,[13] from whom Jesus also traces His lineage.[14] Paul says: "And if you be Christ's, then are you the seed of Abraham, heirs according to the promise" (Gal 3:29). Paul also says: "Therefore is it of faith, that according to grace the promise might be firm to all the seed; not to that only which is of the law, but to that also which is of the faith of Abraham, who is the father of us all" (Rom 4:16).

Why are Christians the seed of Abraham? Because if we have faith in God as Abraham did, we become children of the promise that God made to Abraham — namely, that we would be forever blessed in Jesus Christ.[15] Paul says: "The blessing of Abraham might come on the Gentiles through Christ Jesus: that we may receive the promise of the Spirit by faith."[16] The Blessed Virgin Mary also recounts God's promise to Abraham as she declares: "He hath received Israel his servant, being mindful of his mercy: As he spoke to our fathers, to Abraham and to his seed for ever."[17] Through faith in Christ, the children of Abraham now have access to God's grace in the New Covenant.[18]

---

[13] See Rom 4:12, 16. God made two promises to Abraham. First, to give his descendants a physical dwelling place on earth (Gen 15:18-21). God fulfilled this promise (see Jos 21:43; 2 Esd 9:8 [Neh in RSV-CE]; 3 Kings 8:56 [1 Kings in RSV-CE]). Thus, God owes the Jews nothing more (this refutes the Zionist movement, which seeks a restoration of Israel). Second, to give Abraham and his descendants an eternal dwelling place in heaven (Gen 13:15; 17:7-8; 22:17-18). This promise has been partially fulfilled in the New Covenant, and will be completely fulfilled at the end of the world.

[14] See Mt 1:1-17.

[15] We must remember that Abraham pleased God with his faith *when he was a Gentile* (Gen 12:1-3). Thus, God entered into his first covenant with Abraham, promising him and his descendants an eternal dwelling place, *when he was a Gentile* (Gen 13:15; 17:7-8). This covenant foreshadowed the New Covenant, which, unlike the Mosaic covenant, would also include Gentiles.

[16] Gal 3:14. See also Rom 4:13, 16; 9:8; Gal 3:18-19, 22, 29; 4:28; Eph 3:6; Heb 6:13.

[17] Lk 1:54-55.

[18] See Rom 5:2.

Even though God's covenant with Abraham preceded God's covenant with Moses, we look to the Abrahamic covenant as the prototype of the New Covenant. This is because God's covenant with Abraham was based on personal faith,[19] and God's covenant with Moses was based on impersonal "works of law."[20] Since God's covenant with Abraham was based on faith and His covenant with Moses was not, Jesus transformed the Abrahamic covenant into His New Covenant, and, at the same time, abolished the Mosaic covenant.[21]

In the New Covenant, Jesus fulfills and perfects the Abrahamic covenant as God promised, by giving us access to His grace. Through Christ and the Catholic Church, which is the worldwide family of God, *all the nations shall be blessed*.[22] This transformation of God's covenant with Abraham into the New Covenant of Jesus Christ, who blesses all nations through the Church, connects Peter to Abraham, and underscores their unique roles of covenant leadership. Peter takes the place of Abraham as the rock foundation of the New Israel, the Church.[23] Just as Abraham is the rock from which God's people were hewn, Peter is the rock upon which Christ builds the Church, uniting the children of Abraham into His one body.

The "Peter Is Just a Small Rock" Argument

The previous non-Catholic arguments attempted to prove that Peter (*Petros*) is not the rock (*petra*) upon which Jesus builds His Church. But once the exegetical evidence is weighed, any

---

[19] See, for example, Rom 4:2-3, 9-17; Gal 3:8-9; Heb 11:8-10, 17.

[20] See, for example, Rom 3:20, 28; 4:1-2; 9:31-32; Gal 2:16; 3:11; Eph 2:8-9.

[21] See 2 Cor 3:14; Heb 7:18; 8:13; 10:8-9. God required "faith" to be the basis of His covenant with humanity because it was precisely the *lack* of faith of Adam that brought sin and death to the world (cf. Rom 5:12).

[22] See Gen 12:3; 15:5; Gal 3:8.

[23] See Gal 6:16.

honest non-Catholic would admit that Peter is indeed the rock of the Church. Thus, in order to deny the biblical basis for the office of Peter, non-Catholics have come up with an alternative argument: Peter is just a small rock, and Christ is the real rock of the Church. Since we have already explained that Jesus Christ is indeed the rock of the Church, and that He shares this status with Peter, we will now focus on the "small rock" argument.

Those who argue that Peter is a small rock try to drive a wedge between the Greek words *Petros* and *petra* by giving them different definitions. They say that *Petros* (Peter) means a small stone or pebble, while *petra* (rock) means a massive, immovable rock. They make this argument even though Scripture *never* defines *Petros* as a small rock, and, as we will see, Scripture teaches that *petra* is not exclusively a large, immovable rock. First, let's address why Matthew uses two different words (*Petros* and *petra*) in Matthew 16:18.

As we mentioned above, in the Greek language, nouns have a grammatical gender (we do not have such a rule in the English language). Since *petra* is a feminine noun, Matthew, at the direction of the Holy Spirit, recorded Peter's name as *Petros*, which is a masculine noun. Since Greek requires a masculine noun to describe a man (Peter), Matthew translated *petra* as *Petros*. Therefore, Matthew used *Petros* because the Greek gender rules required him to do so, not because Matthew was trying to distinguish Peter from the rock on which Jesus would build His Church.

The Italian language, which I speak fluently, has the same rule. The word for "rock" in Italian is *pietra*. But, when I say my father's name in Italian (which is Peter), I don't refer to him as Pietra. I call him Pietro. Pietro is a masculine noun that reflects the masculine nature of my father, who is obviously a man. This is why my Italian Bible translates Matthew 16:18 as: "Tu sei *Pietro*, a su questa *pietra* io costruiro' la mia Chiesa" ("You are *Pietro*, and on this *pietra* I will build my Church").

Some Protestant apologists argue that Greek requires words to match in gender when they are identified with one another. Thus, they argue that the masculine noun *Petros* cannot be identified with the feminine noun *petra* because the genders do not match. This rule, however, does not apply to proper nouns. It only applies to nouns, pronouns, adjectives, and articles. For example, in 1 Corinthians 10:4, Paul identifies the masculine proper noun *Christos* with the feminine noun *petra*: "And they drank of the spiritual *rock* that followed them, and the *rock* was Christ."

Further, Scripture does not support the argument that *petra* can only be a massive, immovable rock, and hence, distinguishable from *Petros*. Scripture also associates *petra* with a stone or small rock. For example, both Peter and Paul associate the Greek word *lithos* (stone) with the Greek word *petra* (rock). Paul says: "As it is written: Behold I lay in Sion a stumbling*stone* and a *rock* of scandal; and whosoever believeth in him shall not be confounded" (Rom 9:33). Peter says: "And a *stone* of stumbling, and a *rock* of scandal, to them who stumble at the word, neither do believe, whereunto also they are set" (1 Pet 2:8).[24]

Peter and Paul are referring to the prophecy of Isaiah 8:14-15:

> And he shall be a sanctification to you. But for a *stone* of stumbling, and for a *rock* of offence to the two houses of Israel, for a snare and a ruin to the inhabitants of Jerusalem. And very many of them shall stumble and fall, and shall be broken in pieces, and shall be snared, and taken.

Isaiah is prophesying that the Jewish people will reject their Messiah, Jesus Christ, who is "the stone which the builders rejected."[25] Isaiah describes the coming Messiah with the

---

[24] Because he is the Vicar of Christ, Peter is also a "rock" of scandal to Satan, who will never be able to destroy the Church.

[25] Ps 117(118):22; also see Mt 21:42; Mk 12:10; Lk 20:17; Acts 4:11; 1 Pet 2:7.

metaphors "stone" and "rock," over which the inhabitants of Jerusalem will "stumble and fall" (v. 15). In this case, *petra* cannot be a massive, immovable boulder because men cannot stumble over such a large structure. Instead, *petra* refers to a small stone or rock over which a man could stumble and fall. Therefore, the *petra* in Matthew 16:18 cannot be distinguished from *Petros* on the grounds that *petra* is necessarily an enormous structure.

Some may point out that Isaiah says that those who stumble and fall are also "broken to pieces" (v. 15), thus implying that the *petra* of Isaiah 8:14 is a huge boulder. Such an argument does not explain how the people would stumble over such a large structure. This means that the text cannot be excluding smaller rocks that are causing the stumbling. More importantly, the unbelievers in Isaiah 8:15 are broken into pieces *as a result of their stumbling and falling*, not as the result of being crushed under the weight of a large boulder. Peter and Paul affirm this in their epistles because they *only* refer to the "stumbling and falling" aspect of the metaphor, while excluding the "broken in pieces" aspect. Thus, Peter and Paul interpret the *petra* metaphor of Isaiah 8:14-15 as exclusively a rock that causes stumbling.

Nevertheless, even if non-Catholics insist that *petra* in Matthew 16:18 is a massive stone, their exegesis reveals further problems. As we have seen and will further explore, right after Simon confesses the Father's divine revelation, Jesus blesses him, changes his name to Peter, gives him the keys to the kingdom of heaven and the authority to bind and loose. To argue that Jesus was renaming Simon a small pebble is to conclude that Jesus was attempting to diminish, or even punish Peter, right after Jesus blessed him for confessing the Father's divine revelation. But then, immediately after diminishing Peter, Jesus builds Peter back up by giving him the keys to the kingdom and the authority to bind and loose.

In other words, Jesus would be saying: "Blessed are you, Simon Bar-Jona, for confessing my Father's divine revelation; but you are an insignificant little pebble, and I am the real rock on which I will build my Church. Nevertheless, I will give you the keys to the kingdom of heaven, and whatever you bind and loose on earth will be bound and loosed in heaven." Such an argument does not stand to reason. Moreover, if Matthew really wanted to describe Peter as a small rock, he would have used the word *Lithos* (which, in Greek, means a small pebble). *Lithos*, and not *Petros*, would have been the proper Greek word to use if Matthew wished to emphasize the smallness of Peter's rock stature.

Another important rebuttal to the non-Catholic argument is that Jesus may have actually spoken the words in Matthew 16:18-19 in Aramaic, not Greek.[26] Aramaic had become the language of the Palestinian Jews before the Christian era. Jesus' description of Simon "Bar-Jona" indicates that Jesus was speaking Aramaic when He renamed Simon "rock."[27] In Aramaic, "Bar" means "son," and "Jona" means "John." "Jona" also means "dove," which is the form that the Holy Spirit chose to reveal Himself when He descended upon Jesus.[28] Simon was the son of John, as well as the son of the Holy Spirit, since he received and communicated God's divine revelation.

What does this mean? It means that Jesus would have renamed Simon by calling him *Kepha* (not *Petros*). The word *kepha* is Aramaic for a rock. Unlike nouns in the Greek language, Aramaic nouns are void of gender. Therefore, in the original Aramaic tongue, which the Holy Spirit translated into Greek, there was no

---

[26] Many Catholic apologists assume Jesus spoke Aramaic in Mt 16:18-19, but this cannot be proven definitively. The people of Jesus' time also spoke Greek and Latin. This is demonstrated by the Greek and Latin translations of "The King of the Jews" on the sign that was affixed to Jesus' cross during the Crucifixion (Jn 19:20). Therefore, apologetical arguments should not be based entirely on the assumption that Jesus spoke Aramaic.

[27] See also Mk 15:34, where Jesus speaks Aramaic when he quotes Ps 21:2 (22:1), declaring that He is the Christ: "Eloi, Eloi, lamma sabacthani?"

[28] See Mt 3:16; Mk 1:10; Lk 3:22; Jn 1:32.

grammatical distinction between the rock in the first clause with the rock in the second clause (see Mt 16:18). The use of Aramaic would make Jesus' play on words more emphatic: "You are *Kepha*, and on this *kepha* I will build my church." The connection between Peter and the rock on which Jesus would build the Church would have been crystal clear to those who heard the declaration as it was originally spoken by Jesus.

The Gospels provide evidence that Jesus renamed Simon *Kepha*. As we saw in John 1:42, Jesus calls Simon "Cephas," which is the Greek transliteration of the Aramaic word *Kepha*. As we alluded to, Paul also refers to Peter as "Cephas" in 1 Corinthians 1:12; 3:22; 9:5; 15:5, and Galatians 2:9. Peter is the *Kepha*, or massive stone, on which Jesus builds His Church. If Jesus wanted to distinguish Peter from the "real" rock of the Church, Jesus would have used the word *evna*, which means "little pebble" in Aramaic. *Evna* would have been translated as *lithos*, while *Kepha* would have been translated as *Petros*. This demonstrates that Peter is not a mere "chip off the old rock." Instead, Peter is THE rock on which Jesus builds His Church.

Therefore, Jesus, like the wise man, "built his house upon a rock, and the rain fell, and the floods came, and the winds blew, and they beat upon that house, and it fell not, for it was founded on a rock."[29]

---

[29] Mt 7:24-25; see Lk 6:48.

CHAPTER THREE

—⌁⌁⌁—

Peter Has the Keys to the Kingdom of Heaven

Right after Simon confesses the Father's revelation and Jesus blesses Simon and changes his name to "rock," Jesus declares to Peter: "I will give to thee the keys of the kingdom of heaven" (Mt 16:19). The Greek word for you (*soi*) is singular, which means that Jesus gives the keys to Peter *alone*. Jesus also gives Peter the authority to "bind and loose," which we will discuss later (see Mt 16:19).

Many non-Catholics have an incomplete picture of these terms. Many believe that Peter's binding and loosing authority regarded his ability to let the Gentiles into God's kingdom while he was on earth. Now in heaven, Peter's keys represent his authority to admit or deny people's entrance through the pearly gates.

Sacred Scripture provides us a much different understanding of binding and loosing. In order to truly comprehend the significance of these terms ("rock," "keys of the kingdom," and "bind and loose"), we must put ourselves in the mindset of the first-century Jews. Unlike us twenty-first century Westerners, these Jewish people would have immediately recognized the importance of these terms.

We first recall that Matthew was writing for a Jewish audience. This means Matthew employed terms that would have been familiar to the Jews. In fact, the Catholic Church has held that Matthew composed his Gospel in the Hebrew language as well as the inspired Greek.[1] The primary evidence that Matthew's Gospel was written down in Hebrew comes from Papias (c. A.D. 130), who said that Matthew "composed the oracles in the Hebrew language." Other early Church fathers such as Irenaeus, John Chrysostom, Cyril of Jerusalem, Jerome, and Augustine also allude to Matthew's Gospel as having been written in Hebrew.

It is unclear whether the Holy Spirit inspired Matthew to write all or only parts of his Gospel in Hebrew, in addition to the Greek, or whether the Hebrew was only a translation of the inspired Greek text. But, in any event, it is clear that Matthew's Gospel was held in particular esteem by the Jews of the early Church. This is because Matthew explained to the Jews the New Testament Church through the lens of the Old Testament Scriptures, from which he quotes more than any other evangelist.[2] In other words, Matthew believed in the maxim "Scripture interprets Scripture."

Because Protestants believe the Bible is the only infallible authority, they often employ this same maxim to support their exegesis. We will once again show how using Scripture to interpret Scripture unlocks the meaning of Matthew 16:19 and vindicates the Catholic position. We will do this by first examining the significance of "the keys of the kingdom," and later, the authority to "bind and loose." But before we do, let's put ourselves in the frame of mind of the Jewish people of the first century, to whom Matthew was writing.

The Jewish people of Jesus' time were anxiously waiting for God's Messiah to come and restore the kingdom previously established by King David around 1000 B.C. God established this

---

[1] The Pontifical Biblical Commission of 1911 maintained that Matthew "composed the first gospel in the native language then employed by the Jews of Palestine."

[2] Matthew quotes from the Old Testament no less than sixty-five times.

national kingdom by entering into a covenant with David, whom God describes as "a man according to his own heart."[3] No one else in Scripture is described in this manner. After God established His covenant with David and made him His first king, God promised David that his offspring would be blessed and his throne would be established forever:

> I have made a covenant with my elect: I have sworn to David my servant: Thy seed will I settle for ever. And I will build up thy throne unto generation and generation.[4]

However, not long after its establishment, the Davidic kingdom split into two separate nations that were eventually overtaken by foreign aggressors.[5] This caused the Jews to scatter throughout Palestine. They were no longer united. By the time Jesus had arrived on the scene, the divided kingdom had been almost completely destroyed by foreign invasions and persecutions. But the Jews continued to have faith in God's promise that He would establish David's throne forever.

We need to appreciate how the Jews were yearning for the restoration of their kingdom. The Jews identified themselves as God's favored people because they were descendants of David. As David's offspring, the Jews were rightful heirs of David's kingdom. Once the kingdom was restored by the coming Messiah, the Jews believed they would be free from Roman persecution and exercise their royal dominion over all the nations of the earth.[6]

---

[3] 1 Kings 13:14 (1 Sam in RSV-CE).

[4] Ps 88:4-5 (89:3-4).

[5] See 3 Kings 12:16-20; 14:21-31 (1 Kings in RSV-CE). The kingdom divided into the northern (Israel) and southern (Judah) nations in 931 B.C. Assyria would conquer Israel in 722 B.C., and Babylon would conquer Judah in 586 B.C.

[6] See Ps 2:8.

How would God specifically restore the kingdom? God promised David that He would raise up a king from his lineage who would bring all the nations under the eternal kingship of God. This king would not only be the son of David, but also the Son of God, whose kingdom on earth would be established forever:

> And when thy days shall be fulfilled, and thou shalt sleep with thy fathers, I will raise up thy seed after thee, which shall proceed out of thy bowels, and I will establish his kingdom. He shall build a house to my name, and I will establish the throne of his kingdom for ever. I will be to him a father, and he shall be to me a son: and if he commit any iniquity, I will correct him with the rod of men, and with the stripes of the children of men.[7]

God repeats His promise to David through Nathan in the following passage:

> And when thou shalt have ended thy days to go to thy fathers, I will raise up thy seed after thee, which shall be of thy sons: and I will establish his kingdom. He shall build me a house, and I will establish his throne for ever. I will be to him a father, and he shall be to me a son: and I will not take my mercy away from him, as I took it from him that was before thee. But I will settle him in my house, and in my kingdom for ever: and his throne shall be most firm for ever. According to all these words, and according to all this vision, so did Nathan speak to David.[8]

The Jews certainly had something to be excited about. God promised to establish for them an everlasting monarchy through a descendant of David, whose throne would last forever. Once

---

[7] 2 Kings 7:12-14 (2 Sam in RSV-CE).
[8] 1 Para 17:11-15 (1 Chron in RSV-CE).

their kingdom was restored, the Jews believed that God would free them from their enemies and grant them prosperity, security, and everlasting happiness. Even after the Davidic kingdom split and was given over to pagan nations, God sent many prophets to affirm His promise that the righteous one from David's lineage would restore the kingdom of David.

For example:

- "Behold the days come, saith the Lord, and I will raise up to David a just branch: and a king shall reign, and shall be wise, and shall execute judgment and justice in the earth" (Jer 23:5).
- "For thus saith the Lord: There shall not be cut off from David a man to sit upon the throne of the house of Israel" (Jer 33:17).
- "But in the days of those kingdoms the God of heaven will set up a kingdom that shall never be destroyed, and his kingdom shall not be delivered up to another people, and it shall break in pieces, and shall consume all these kingdoms, and itself shall stand for ever" (Dan 2:44).

The sacred writers of the New Testament made it clear that Jesus is this King from the line of David who had come to restore and perfect the Davidic kingdom as the worldwide household of God. For example:

- Matthew opens his Gospel by tracing Jesus' royal pedigree back to David: "The book of the generation of Jesus Christ, the son of David."[9]
- The angel Gabriel reveals to Mary: "He shall be great, and shall be called the Son of the most High; and the Lord God shall give unto him the throne of David his father;

---

[9] Mt 1:1; see also Lk 3:31.

and he shall reign in the house of Jacob for ever. And of his
kingdom there shall be no end."[10]
- The angel of the Lord declares to the Jewish shepherds:
"For, this day, is born to you a Saviour, who is Christ the
Lord, in the city of David" (Lk 2:11).
- Nathanael declares to Jesus: "Rabbi, thou art the Son of
God, thou art the king of Israel" (Jn 1:49).
- Many others also recognized Jesus' special status as the
long-awaited "son of David."[11]

This brief background helps us understand how sensitive the
Jewish people would have been to Jesus' words, which He carefully
chose to communicate His message. When Jesus, the proclaimed
son of David and king of Israel, gave Peter the "keys to the kingdom," most Jews would have immediately recognized that Jesus
was referring to the Davidic kingdom, which He came to restore.
They would have also recognized that Jesus was appointing Peter,
the new rock of God's covenant family, to be the chief steward (or
prime minister) of His kingdom.

In the kingdom of David, the king who sat on David's throne
would delegate his authority to a chief steward who would rule
and govern in the king's absence. The king would formally invest
the chief steward with this power by giving him the "keys to the
kingdom." As the keeper of the keys, the chief steward (also called
"vizier" or "majordomo" or "chamberlain") was said to be "over the
house" of the king. The chief steward would be second only to the
king, and would have plenary authority over the palace and the
ability to render judgments over the king's subjects.

When Jesus, the rightful heir to the throne of David, gave
Peter the "keys to the kingdom," the Jews would have instantly

[10] Lk 1:32-33.
[11] Mt 9:27; 15:22; 20:30-31; Mk 10:47-48; Lk 18:38-39.

recognized that Jesus was restoring the Davidic kingdom and appointing Peter "over the house" of God. In fact, the Jewish Scriptures mention "keys" in the context of a "kingdom" only one time: *in describing the authority of the Davidic king's chief steward.* We now examine this important passage in Isaiah.

Eliakim Has the Keys to the Kingdom

In Isaiah 22:15-23, God describes the state of the Davidic kingdom in around the year 715 B.C. At this time in history, Hezekiah (Ezechias) was the king, and Shebna (Sobna) was his chief steward. Through the prophet Isaiah, God reveals that He will remove Shebna from his office and replace him with Eliakim (Eliacim), to whom He gives the "key of the house of David":

> Thus saith the Lord God of hosts: Go, get thee in to him that dwelleth in the tabernacle, to Sobna who is over the temple: and thou shalt say to him: What dost thou here, or as if thou wert somebody here? for thou hast hewed thee out a sepulchre here, thou hast hewed out a monument carefully in a high place, a dwelling for thyself in a rock. . . . And I will drive thee out from thy station, and depose thee from thy ministry. And it shall come to pass in that day, that I will call my servant Eliacim the son of Helcias, and I will clothe him with thy robe, and will strengthen him with thy girdle, and will give thy power into his hand: and he shall be as a father to the inhabitants of Jerusalem, and to the house of Juda. And I will lay the key of the house of David upon his shoulder: and he shall open, and none shall shut: and he shall shut, and none shall open. And I will fasten him as a peg in a sure place, and he shall be for a throne of glory to the house of his father.

In the first two verses, God reveals that Shebna is the chief steward of the kingdom by describing him as "over the temple" (v. 15) of David, who has made a dwelling for himself "in a rock" (v. 16). The "temple" or "house" was the king's palace, and the chief steward was the administrator or chamberlain of the palace. The Scriptures use this phrase "over the temple" or "over the house" (in Hebrew, *al habayith*) to describe the king's chief steward or major-domo in a variety of places. For example:

- Ahishar was the "governor of the house" of King Solomon (the first recorded instance of *al habayith*).[12]
- Arza was over the house of King Elah.[13]
- Obadiah was over the house of King Ahab.[14]
- An unnamed steward was over the house of King Joram.[15]
- Azrikam was the "governor of the house" of Maaseiah.[16]
- Mordecai was "over the house" of Esther.[17]

The chief steward over the Davidic household would not only regulate the affairs of the king's palace, but also render judgments over the people of Israel in the king's absence. For example, when God struck down King Azariah, his chief steward Jotham "governed the palace, and judged the people of the land."[18] The king's authority to judge was delegated to the one who was "over the house."

Notwithstanding Shebna's exalted position in Israel's royal monarchy, God declares that He will remove Shebna from his "station" and "ministry" (v. 19). God will replace Shebna with a

---

[12] See 3 Kings 4:6.

[13] See 3 Kings 16:9.

[14] See 3 Kings 18:3.

[15] See 4 Kings 10:5 (2 Kings in RSV-CE).

[16] See 2 Para 28:7 (2 Chron in RSV-CE).

[17] See Esther 8:2. King Herod also had a chief steward. See Lk 8:3 (named "Chusa") and Acts 12:20 (named "Blastus").

[18] 4 Kings 15:5; see also 2 Para 26:21.

new chief steward, Eliakim, elevating him to the royal office or station (see v. 20). God transfers Shebna's power to Eliakim, and clothes him with Shebna's robe and girdle (see v. 21). Eliakim will now be known as a "father" to Israel (see v. 21).

Further, to officially install Eliakim to the station of chief steward, God gives him the "key" of the house of David, which was previously held by Shebna (see v. 22). As we saw in the Old Testament Scriptures, the "house of David" means the "kingdom" that God promised to establish forever.[19] As the keeper of the keys, whatever Eliakim opens, no one will shut; and whatever he shuts, no one will open (see v. 22). This refers to the authority that Eliakim exercises on behalf of the king. Eliakim is second only to King Hezekiah and has complete dominion over the kingdom.

Eliakim's appointment "over the house" of David was a significant reminder to the Jews of their royal heritage. God had always been directly involved with the administration of His kingdom. This included effecting the appointments of kings and chief stewards to their perpetual offices. When God installed Eliakim, the Davidic kingdom was 300 years old and Hezekiah was its fourteenth king. The kingdom was preserved through an unbroken succession of kings and chief stewards. Through God's divine protection and guidance, the Jews knew that God would fulfill His promise of establishing the kingdom forever.

When we let Scripture interpret Scripture, the parallels between Isaiah 22 (the kingdom of God foreshadowed) and Matthew 16 (the kingdom of God fulfilled) are self-evident:

- Shebna's dwelling is compared to a "rock" / Peter is also called "rock."
- Shebna is "over the house" / Peter, by virtue of the keys, is also "over the house."

---

[19] See 2 Kings 7:12-13 and 1 Para 17:11-12.

- Eliakim succeeds to Shebna's perpetual "station" and "ministry" / Linus succeeds to Peter's perpetual office.[20]
- Shebna's power is transferred to Eliakim / Peter's power is transferred to Linus.
- Eliakim is a "father" to the inhabitants of Jerusalem / Peter and his successors are "fathers" to the inhabitants of the New Jerusalem, the Church.
- God gives Eliakim the keys to the kingdom / Jesus gives Peter the keys to the kingdom.
- Eliakim has the authority to open and shut / Peter has the authority to bind and loose.
- Eliakim succeeds to his office like "a peg in a sure place" / Peter succeeds to his office as the "rock."

No educated Jew, who would have been familiar with these words from the prophet Isaiah, would have missed the profound implication of Jesus' words in Matthew 16. Having heard these words of Isaiah proclaimed in the temple for over seven hundred years, the Jewish people would have immediately made the connection between Hezekiah and Eliakim, between Jesus and Peter. They would have recognized that Jesus was restoring the Davidic kingdom and declaring Himself to be the king. They would have also recognized that Jesus, on the basis of scriptural and legal precedent, was delegating His authority to Peter, his chief steward, by giving him the keys to the kingdom.

Why did Jesus need to delegate His authority to Peter? Because Jesus would be leaving His apostles and would need a chief steward over His earthly kingdom. This is demonstrated by what Jesus tells His apostles *immediately after* He promises Peter the keys. *For the very first time*, Jesus tells His apostles that He is going to be put to death: "From that time Jesus began to shew to

---

[20] Linus was the first successor to Peter in A.D. 67 and is mentioned in 2 Tim 4:21.

his disciples, that he must go to Jerusalem, and suffer many things from the ancients and scribes and chief priests, and be put to death, and the third day rise again."[21]

Jesus revealed His death and resurrection precisely at this time to explain why He was giving Peter the keys. After the consummation of the paschal mystery, King Jesus would no longer be visibly present in the kingdom He was restoring. Jesus would need a prime minister to act on His behalf, whose authority would be represented by "the keys."

But with the inauguration of the New Covenant, the temporal kingdom of Israel would become the eternal kingdom of God. The national kingdom of David would become the universal kingdom of the Catholic Church. The office of chief steward would become the office of Peter, represented by the keys of the kingdom and the authority to bind (shut) and loose (open).

What Is the Significance of King Hezekiah?

Why did God pick the reign of King Hezekiah, as opposed to some other king, to reveal the succession of chief stewards? Because, according to Jewish tradition, Hezekiah was the king who most closely prefigured the Messiah, Jesus Christ. Remember that God promised to establish the Davidic throne forever by sending His Messiah as King. Therefore, each Davidic king foreshadowed their coming Messiah.[22] When God would finally send His true Messiah, He would perfect the Davidic kingdom by saving the people of Israel from their iniquity.[23]

God also revealed to the people of Israel that their Messiah would be put to death and rise again on the third day. Hosea prophesied: "He will revive us after two days: on the third day he

---

[21] Mt 16:21; see also Mt 17:21-22; Jn 13:33; 14:2.
[22] See Is 33:17, 22.
[23] See Is 33:24.

will raise us up, and we shall live in his sight."[24] The Jews believed that their Messianic "King of the world will raise us up, who die for his laws, in the resurrection of eternal life."[25]

What does this have to do with Hezekiah foreshadowing Jesus Christ? God decreed Hezekiah' death, and then raised him up on the third day, just as He did with Jesus. When King Hezekiah was "sick unto death" and the Lord told him, "Thou shalt die, and not live,"[26] Hezekiah beseeched the Lord to save him with prayer and weeping.[27] God answered him: "I have heard thy prayer, and I have seen thy tears: and behold I have healed thee; *on the third day* thou shalt go up to the temple of the Lord."[28] Therefore, Hezekiah, more than any other Davidic king, prefigured the Messiah who would die and rise again.[29]

By raising Hezekiah on the third day, God made Hezekiah an important Messianic figure. Because Hezekiah foreshadowed the Messiah, Hezekiah's kingdom foreshadowed the Messiah's kingdom. Because Hezekiah had a succession of chief stewards, Jesus would also have a succession of chief stewards. Because Hezekiah and Jesus are so closely connected, Eliakim and Peter are closely connected. Jesus is the new Hezekiah and Peter is the new Eliakim. Peter's keys represent royal authority over the kingdom of God, which Jesus left Peter to govern while He was in heaven. Jesus came not to abolish the Old Covenant kingdom, but to fulfill it.[30]

Because Eliakim's appointment as chief steward under the reign of Hezekiah was so important, God reveals it in many places

---

[24] Osee 6:3 (Hos in RSV-CE).

[25] 2 Mac 7:9; See also Soph 3:8 (Zeph in RSV-CE); 2 Mac 7:14; 12:43.

[26] 4 Kings 20:1.

[27] See 4 Kings 20:2-3.

[28] 4 Kings 20:5; see also 4 Kings 20:8.

[29] Further, of the twenty kings of Judah, only Hezekiah, David, and Josiah were righteous in the eyes of God (see Ecclesiasticus 45:9 [Sirach in RSV-CE]).

[30] See Mt 5:17.

throughout Scripture. Notice also how Eliakim is described as "over the house" and his name always appears before the other palace officials. Here are some examples:

- "And they called for the king: and there went out to them *Eliacim* the son of Helcias who was over the house, and Sobna the scribe, and Joahe the son of Asaph the recorder."[31]
- "And *Eliacim* the son of Helcias, who was over the house, and Sobna the scribe, and Joahe the son of Asaph the recorder, came to Ezechias, with their garments rent, and told him the words of Rabsaces."[32]
- "And he sent *Eliacim*, who was over the house, and Sobna the scribe, and the ancients of the priests covered with sackcloths, to Isaias the prophet the son of Amos."[33]
- "And there went out to him *Eliacim* the son of Helcias, who was over the house, and Sobna the scribe, and Joahe the son of Asaph the recorder."[34]

Doesn't Jesus Have the Keys of the New Covenant Kingdom?

To deny the obvious link between Isaiah 22 and Matthew 16, non-Catholics argue that the key in Isaiah is different from the keys in Matthew. One way they do this is to point out that Isaiah uses the phrase "key of the house of David" and Matthew uses "keys to the kingdom of heaven."

Because the terminology is different, they argue that Isaiah was referring to the earthly house of David, but Matthew is referring to the heavenly kingdom of Christ. In other words, even

---

[31] 4 Kings 18:18.
[32] 4 Kings 18:37; see also Is 36:22
[33] 4 Kings 19:2; see also Is 37:2
[34] Is 36:3.

though both Isaiah 22 and Matthew 16 use "keys" in the context of exercising earthly authority (binding/loosing; opening/shutting), Protestants argue that Jesus' use of "kingdom of heaven" in Matthew 16 really means the heavenly beatitude. That would mean Jesus was appointing Peter to be a mere celestial gatekeeper for those entering eternal paradise.

Such an argument shows to what lengths Protestants will go to deny Peter's authority and the plain meaning of Scripture. Isaiah 22 is about the *earthly* kingdom of David. It is the *only* Scriptural precedent for using "keys" in connection with "binding and loosing" (opening/shutting), the same terms Jesus uses in Matthew 16. Moreover, Jesus tells Peter, "Whatsoever thou shalt bind *upon earth*, it shall be bound also in heaven" (v. 19). Jesus is referring to His *earthly* kingdom because Peter will bind and loose *on earth*. This New Covenant kingdom in Matthew 16 will replace the Old Covenant kingdom of Isaiah 22, as the prophets revealed.

While Isaiah 22 uses "house of David" and Matthew 16 uses "kingdom," this does not mean that the "kingdom" of Matthew 16 is a reference to something other than Christ's earthly kingdom, the Church. David himself uses the term "kingdom" to describe his earthly empire: "And among my sons (for the Lord hath given me many sons) he hath chosen Solomon my son, to sit upon the throne of the *kingdom of the Lord* over Israel."[35] The terms "house" and "kingdom" refer to the same institution.

In light of these and other Old Testament precedents, Jesus frequently used the word "kingdom" to describe the *earthly* kingdom of God, which is the Catholic Church. For example, Jesus says:

- "The *kingdom of heaven* is like to a grain of mustard seed . . . when it is grown up, it is greater than all herbs, and

---

[35] 1 Para 28:5; see also 1 Para 29:23.

becometh a tree, so that the birds of the air come, and dwell in the branches thereof."[36]

- "The *kingdom of heaven* is likened to a man that sowed good seeds in his field. But while men were asleep, his enemy came and oversowed cockle among the wheat and went his way."[37]

- "The *kingdom of heaven* is like to leaven, which a woman took and hid in three measures of meal, until the whole was leavened" (Mt 13:33).

- "Again the *kingdom of heaven* is like to a net cast into the sea, and gathering together of all kind of fishes" (Mt 13:47).

- "Then shall the *kingdom of heaven* be like to ten virgins, who taking their lamps went out to meet the bridegroom and the bride. And five of them were foolish, and five wise."[38]

In each of these cases, the "kingdom of heaven" describes the Church on earth, not the eternal state of glory. The kingdom of heaven (the Church) is like a mustard seed that grows into a large tree, like bread that is leavened, and like a net that catches fish of every kind. These metaphors are describing the earthly Church, which changes over time, not the heavenly city, which is eternal and unchanging. When Jesus describes the kingdom of heaven as composed of "bad seeds" and "fools," He can only be describing the Church on earth, not the state of heavenly bliss (since there are no bad seeds or fools in heaven, but plenty in the Church on earth!). Thus, when Jesus gave Peter the keys to the "kingdom of heaven," Jesus was appointing him *over the kingdom of God on earth* (not the celestial kingdom of heaven).

---

[36] Mt 13:31-32; see also Mk 4:31-32; Lk 13:19.

[37] Mt 13:24-25.

[38] Mt 25:1-2.

These metaphors for the earthly Church also remind us that she is a living organism — namely, Christ's body. This means that her appearance changes during the course of her existence, but her essence remains the same. The Church of the twenty-first century does not externally resemble the Church of the first century, but it is organically *the same Church*. This is analogous to the human body, which looks much different in its elderly years than it did as an infant. While its appearance has changed, it is the same body.

Another way non-Catholics try to distinguish Eliakim's "key" in Isaiah from Peter's "keys" in Matthew is by pointing out Jesus' statement in the Apocalypse (Revelation): "These things saith the Holy One and the true one, he that hath *the key of David*; he that openeth, and no man shutteth; shutteth, and no man openeth" (Apoc 3:7). Because Jesus in Matthew uses "keys" in the plural, and the Apocalypse and Isaiah use "key" in the singular, the non-Catholic concludes that Jesus did not give Peter the "key" to the house of David, the restored kingdom of God.

This is another weak attempt to create a distinction between Jesus' keys and Peter's keys without any biblical basis for doing so. The Catholic could just as easily argue that since the Apocalypse uses the phrase "key of David" and Isaiah uses the more extensive phrase "key of the house of David," they are different keys. Grammatically speaking, this would not preclude Jesus from giving Peter the "key of the house of David" as part of the "keys to the kingdom," while retaining the "key of David" for Himself.

So why did Jesus give Peter "keys" (plural) when Isaiah only mentions a "key" (singular)? Because, *in addition* to the key of David, Jesus *also* gave Peter the keys of death and hell. In the Apocalypse, Jesus says:

- "Fear not. I am the First and the Last, and alive, and was dead, and behold I am living for ever and ever, and have the *keys of death and of hell*" (Apoc 1:17-18).

John also sees an angel holding a similar key:

- "And the fifth angel sounded the trumpet, and I saw a star fall from heaven upon the earth, and there was given to him the *key of the bottomless pit*" (Apoc 9:1).
- John further reveals: "And I saw an angel coming down from heaven, having the *key of the bottomless pit*, and a great chain in his hand" (Apoc 20:1).

The "keys of death and hell" represent Jesus' authority over life and death. The word "hell" (in Greek, *Hades*) refers to the place of the dead prior to Jesus' resurrection.[39] Hades was the place where all souls, both the righteous and the unrighteous, were detained immediately after death. No soul could go to heaven until Jesus appeased God's wrath against sin by His propitiatory sacrifice, and was raised from the dead.

By virtue of His death and resurrection, God gave Jesus the "keys of death and hell," which represents Jesus' power to release these souls from Hades. This is why, immediately after He died, Jesus "descended into hell" and preached the Gospel to the souls in Hades.[40] The righteous souls could now be released to heaven, while the unrighteous souls were condemned to eternal punishment. The gates of hell, which formerly kept souls from heaven, can no longer do so because Jesus has the keys.

In Matthew 16, Jesus gives Peter these keys of death and hell. By doing so, Jesus gives Peter the authority over souls. Because Peter is the rock of the Church who holds the "keys of death and hell," the gates of hell will not prevail against the Church. Peter has the keys to unlock them. This is precisely why, right after Jesus

---

[39] See, for example, Acts 2:27, 31; 1 Cor 15:55. *Hades* was like a temporary holding cell and is to be distinguished from *Gehenna*, which is the place of the eternally damned, which we call "hell." See, for example, Mt 5:22, 29-30; 10:28; 18:9; 23:15; Mk 9:42, 44, 46; Lk 12:5.

[40] See Lk 16:22-23; Eph 4:8-9; 1 Pet 3:19; 4:6; see also the Apostles' Creed.

promises to build His Church upon Peter, He says that "the *gates of hell* shall not prevail against it" (v. 18).

Why will the gates of hell attack the Church? Because (1) its supernatural powers seek to keep souls out of heaven, and (2) the Church is the caretaker of souls. Just as the gates of hell detained souls before Jesus' resurrection, these dark forces continue to try and prevent souls from entering heaven after His resurrection. But Peter's "keys" fit into the "gates" of hell, which means that Peter has dominion over them. Through Peter's teaching authority, souls will receive the truth of Jesus Christ and will have free access to heaven, uninhibited by the gates of hell.

Thus, Peter not only has the "key of the house of David," but also the "key of death and hell." This is why Jesus gave Peter "keys" (plural) in Matthew 16:19. We should remember that, in the New Testament, "keys" are metaphors for authority. The "key of the house of David" represents Peter's authority over Church governance. Just like the palace administrators of the Davidic kingdom, Peter regulates all the affairs of the kingdom-Church. The "keys of death and hell" represent Peter's authority over the supernatural. This includes the power to forgive and retain sins, and the authority to render infallible decrees (which we will discuss further in the next section).

These different aspects of Peter's authority are not mutually exclusive. Just as the Church is one on earth as it is in heaven, Peter's rule over the Church concerns the temporal as well as the eternal. For example, the consequences of Peter's authority to excommunicate a heretic from the Church may be temporal if the heretic repents (Peter "opens" or "looses"), or eternal if the heretic dies without repenting (Peter "shuts" or "binds"). The "key of David" and the "keys of death and hell" represent different aspects of Peter's divine authority, whose source is Jesus Christ.

The "key to the bottomless pit" seen by John is another metaphor for Jesus' supernatural authority. Just as Jesus can release souls to heaven (with the key of death and Hades), He can also cast souls into Gehenna (with the key of the bottomless pit). "Bottomless" refers to the eternal nature of the pit it describes, which is a metaphor for the place of the damned. Just as Jesus symbolically gives this key to His angel, He has also given this key to Peter, His Vicar.[41] If people separate themselves from the teachings of the Vicar of Christ, they will be condemned. Thus, Jesus' "keys of death and hell" either open the gates to the "kingdom of heaven" (salvation) or the "bottomless pit" (damnation). These "keys" are multiple metaphors for the same supernatural authority.

Delegation, Not Relinquishment

Remember, the king never relinquishes his authority. Jesus is the King to whom the Father has given all authority.[42] Jesus' authority is not undermined by His own decision to give Peter the keys. Jesus is still the primary holder of the keys, and Peter is the secondary holder by delegation. This is why Jesus says "my Church" and "my sheep," even though He has delegated His authority over the Church and the sheep to Peter.[43] Jesus is still in charge of the Church, and He will come to reclaim the keys of His kingdom at the end of the world. At that time, He will "remove the peg that was fastened in a sure place," as He promised.[44]

Jesus revealed in many parables about how He (the Master of the house) would leave His property to stewards, and then reclaim it at the end of time. For example, Jesus tells the story about the householder who planted a vineyard and lent it out to stewards

---

[41] It is not surprising to see an angel with Jesus' key to the bottomless pit. Scripture teaches that God uses angels to bring about His judgment upon evil doers (see, for example, Mt 13:39, 41, 49; 16:27; Mk 8:38; Lk 12:9).

[42] See Mt 28:18.

[43] See Jn 21:15-17.

[44] See Is 22:25.

while he sojourned to a foreign country.[45] The householder is a metaphor for God and the vineyard is a metaphor for the Church. God entrusts the vineyard to His stewards for a period of time and then returns to render an account of their service.

Jesus tells a similar story about the servants and talents, where the householder delegated the stewards his goods and went to a faraway country.[46] When the householder returned, he rendered judgment. Those servants who used their talents were rewarded with salvation, and those who did not were condemned.

Immediately after this parable, Jesus declares how He will judge the entire world based on our works (feeding the hungry, clothing the naked) when He comes in glory at the end of time.[47] Some will receive everlasting life, and others everlasting punishment. It is noteworthy how Jesus first discusses the conduct of his stewards (the prelates of the Church) and then the conduct of everyone else (the lay faithful), but both in the context of eternal judgment. This is because the stewards of the house, beginning with the pope, have the greatest accountability to God. Peter, who was most accountable to Jesus, knew this all too well when he said: "For the time is, that judgment should *begin* at the house of God. And if *first at us*, what shall be the end of them that believe not the gospel of God?" (1 Pet 4:17).

Jesus also teaches that the Lord appoints a steward over his family while He is away.[48] The steward is responsible for taking care of the family, including feeding them in due season. The steward is charged with the gravest of responsibilities. If he is unfaithful to his duties, God will cast him out with the hypocrites, where there will be weeping and gnashing of teeth.

---

[45] See Mt 21:33-44; Mk 12:1-11; Lk 20:9-18.
[46] See Mt 25:14-30; see also Lk 19:11-27; 16:1-10.
[47] See Mt 25:31-46.
[48] See Mt 24:43-51.

In Luke's Gospel, Jesus tells another story about servants over the household while their lord is away.[49] After this story, Peter, the one Jesus would choose to be the steward over His house, asks Jesus whether the parable was for the apostles or everyone (see Lk 12:41). Jesus, perhaps with a bit of light-hearted frustration, rhetorically confirms to Peter that he is indeed the steward of the parable: "Who (thinkest thou) is the faithful and wise steward, whom his lord setteth over his family, to give them their measure of wheat in due season?" (Lk 12:42).

Jesus' delegation of the keys to Peter underscores the fact that this is a *divine* appointment. Jesus, the Son of God, is the one conferring the keys upon Peter, just as God was the one conferring the keys upon Eliakim. Even though Jesus is the true holder of the keys, He will ask Peter to exercise the power of the keys as His Vicar on earth. Peter, and not the Bible, will be the unifying force for the Christian community, just as Christ was while He was on earth.

A Comparison Between Joseph and Peter

Just as with Peter and Eliakim, there are also striking parallels between Peter and another Old Testament figure, Joseph. We read about Joseph in the book of Genesis. Joseph was the favored son of Jacob and great-grandson of Abraham, who was sold by his brothers into slavery in Egypt (see Gen 37:28). Although he was a slave, God gave Joseph the ability to interpret dreams, and destined Joseph for greatness.[50]

One evening, Pharaoh, the ruler of Egypt, had a dream that troubled him greatly.[51] Struck with fear, Pharaoh sent for the wise men and interpreters of Egypt to interpret his dream, but none

---

[49] See Lk 12:36-40.

[50] Joseph recognized his ability to interpret dreams infallibly when he said: "Doth not interpretation belong to God?" (Gen 40:8).

[51] See Gen 41:1-8.

were able to do so (see Gen 41:8). Pharaoh was then advised that a Hebrew slave and prisoner named Joseph would be able to interpret the dream. At Pharaoh's command, Joseph was released from prison and brought to Pharaoh. Pharaoh told Joseph his dream and asked Joseph to interpret it.[52] Joseph interpreted the dream, revealing that a famine would strike the land of Egypt, and advising Pharaoh to appoint a wise man to prepare accordingly.[53]

Pharaoh was so pleased with the wisdom of Joseph that he made Joseph the vizier of his kingdom by appointing him "over his house":

> And he said to them: Can we find such another man, that is full of the spirit of God? He said therefore to Joseph: Seeing God hath shewn thee all that thou hast said, can I find one wiser and one like unto thee? Thou shalt be *over my house*, and at the commandment of thy mouth all the people shall obey: only in the kingly throne will I be above thee.[54]

Pharaoh asked his stewards and Joseph a question that only could be answered by divine revelation. Only Joseph answered correctly. Joseph received the revelation from God the Father and communicated it to Pharaoh. In response, Pharaoh appointed Joseph to be the chief steward over his house. Joseph's royal appointment was based entirely on his infallible declaration to King Pharaoh. Sound familiar?

Pharaoh went on to say to Joseph:

> "Behold, I have set you over the whole land of Egypt." Then Pharaoh took his signet ring from his hand and put it on Joseph's hand, and arrayed him in garments of fine linen, and put a gold chain about his neck; and he made

---

[52] See Gen 41:17-24.

[53] See Gen 41:25-36.

[54] Gen 41:38-40; see also Ps 104(105):21-22.

him to ride in his second chariot; and they cried before him, "Bow the knee!" Thus he set him over all the land of Egypt. Moreover Pharaoh said to Joseph: "I am Pharaoh, and without your consent no man shall lift up hand or foot in all the land of Egypt." And Pharaoh called Joseph's name *Zaphenath-paneah*; and he gave him in marriage Asenath, the daughter of Potiphera priest of On. So Joseph went out over the land of Egypt.[55]

After appointing Joseph over his house and the land of Egypt, Pharaoh gave Joseph his own ring as a sign of his authority, as well as a gold chain and a silk robe. The signet ring of authority in the Egyptian kingdom corresponded to the keys of authority in the Davidic kingdom. Pharaoh also gave Joseph a chariot, which enabled Joseph to rule and govern the people of Egypt, and all the people would bow before him.

Pharaoh delegated absolute plenary authority to Joseph to rule over Egypt. Joseph, formerly a slave, was now second in power only to the throne of Pharaoh. By virtue of his royal appointment, Joseph had the authority regulate the affairs of the kingdom. Just as the chief steward in the Davidic kingdom had the authority to "open and shut," Joseph had the authority so that no one could "lift up hand or foot in all the land of Egypt" (v. 44). Because Joseph's status and mission had now changed, Pharaoh changed Joseph's name to *Zaphenath-paneah* (which means "savior of the world" in Egyptian) (see v. 45). Pharaoh further gave Joseph a bride named Asenath, and Joseph commenced his rule over the land of Egypt (see v. 45).

The parallels between Joseph and Peter are remarkable:

---

[55] Gen 41:41-45 (RSV-CE); ancient Egypt was founded as a state about two thousand years before the Davidic kingdom. As such, it served as a blueprint for how Israel would implement its own royal monarchy. In fact, the people of Israel begged God for a king so that they could be like the other nations. See 1 Kings 8:4-5; 19-20.

- They both are asked a question by a king.
- They both receive a divine revelation from God.
- They both answer the king with an infallible declaration.
- They both are appointed by a king over his kingdom and subjects.
- They both receive a sign from the king of their royal authority.[56]
- Both of their names are changed by a king.
- They both are called "father" of their people.[57]
- They both are given a bride.[58]
- They both were brought from slavery to freedom by a king.[59]

These parallels are not mere coincidence. When we let Scripture interpret Scripture, we see another biblical precedent for the royal appointment of Peter as the steward of Jesus' kingdom. The New Testament is concealed in the Old, and the Old Testament is revealed in the New. God's revelation builds upon itself, and the revelations in the New Testament must be interpreted in light of the revelations that preceded it. When we put ourselves in the mindset of the first-century Jews, steeped in the Jewish Scriptures and the monarchical society of their times, we see how the appointments of Joseph and Eliakim foreshadowed Peter's appointment over the kingdom of God.

---

[56] King Pharaoh gave Joseph a signet ring, and King Jesus gave Peter the keys to the kingdom. The pope also wears a signet ring and robe as a sign of his authority, just as Joseph did.

[57] See Gen 45:8.

[58] King Pharaoh gave Joseph the bride Asenath, and King Jesus gave Peter the bride, the Church.

[59] King Pharaoh brought Joseph out of the slavery of Egypt, and King Jesus brought Peter, an uneducated fisherman, out of the slavery of sin.

CHAPTER FOUR

⸺◈⸺

Peter Has the Authority
to Bind and Loose

After Jesus invests Peter with the keys to the kingdom, He declares to Peter: "And whatsoever thou shalt bind upon earth, it shall be bound also in heaven: and whatsoever thou shalt loose on earth, it shall be loosed also in heaven" (Mt 16:19). This language clearly parallels the language that God used when He conferred the keys upon Eliakim: "And I will lay the key of the house of David upon his shoulder: and he shall open, and none shall shut: and he shall shut, and none shall open" (Is 22:22).

Just as Eliakim had the authority to "open and shut," Peter has the authority to "bind and loose." Further, since this authority comes from the keys which Peter alone holds, Jesus delegates to Peter alone the authority to bind (in Greek, *deses*, which is singular "you") and loose (*luses*, singular "you"). (We will address the apostles' authority to bind and loose in Matthew 18:18 later in this discussion.)

What do these terms mean? "Binding and loosing" (in Hebrew, *asar ve-hittar*) were common rabbinical terms used by the Jewish religious authorities of the day. These terms described their legislative and judicial authority to "forbid" or "permit." This included establishing rules of conduct (in Hebrew, *halakah*) for God's people, as well as issuing definitive interpretations of Scripture, oral tradition, and the whole of the Mosaic law. In short, the terms described the Pharisees' authority over doctrinal and disciplinary matters.

Because the Jews are so familiar with these terms, Jesus uses them in Matthew 16:19. In so doing, Jesus is communicating to the Jews, *in their own language*, that He is implementing a new regime. There will be a transfer of power from the teachers of the Law to the teachers of the "law of Christ" (Gal 6:2). The New Covenant of grace will annul the Old Covenant of law, and the chair of Moses will be replaced with the chair of Peter.

Jesus refers to Moses' "chair" and the Pharisees' "binding and loosing" authority in Matthew's Gospel:

> The scribes and the Pharisees have sitten on the *chair* of Moses. All things therefore whatsoever they shall say to you, observe and do: but according to their works do ye not; for they say, and do not. For they *bind* heavy and insupportable burdens, and lay them on men's shoulders; but with a finger of their own they will not *move* them.[1]

First, a word about Moses. God gave Moses a revelation when he was standing near a mammoth rock (Mount Sinai).[2] Moses received and communicated this revelation as God directed.[3] As a result, God appointed Moses over the house of Israel, and He gave him authority over His covenant people.[4] God communicated with Moses on a regular basis and protected Moses from teaching error.[5] God also directed Moses to hand on his authority to successors. Again, sound familiar?

In Jesus' time, the scribes and Pharisees were the successors of Moses and the official teachers of Israel. The "chair of Moses" that Jesus refers to represented their authority to interpret and expound the Mosaic law. The chair would be placed in the middle of the

---

[1] Mt 23:2-4.
[2] See, for example, Ex 19-20.
[3] See, for example, Ex 35; Dt 5.
[4] See, for example, Ex 19:5-6; Dt 7:12-15.
[5] See Ex, Lev, Num, Deut.

synagogue and the authoritative teacher of the Law would sit in the chair to read from Scripture and address the assembly.

The use of the chair of Moses was a development of the oral Jewish tradition (which demonstrates that the Jews did not follow "Scripture alone"). The Jews based their tradition on Exodus 18, where God says: "And the next day Moses sat, to judge the people" (v. 13). Moses rendered God's judgments from his chair: "And Moses answered him: The people come to me to seek the judgment of God. And when any controversy falleth out among them, they come to me to judge between them, and to shew the precepts of God, and his laws" (vv. 15-16).

The authority of Moses and the tradition of his chair were passed down through the ages to Joshua, the elders, the prophets, and finally to the Sanhedrin of Jesus' time. God would give special graces to the one who sat in the chair of Moses, so that Israel would have access to God's infallible judgments (even through their fallible leaders). We have seen this with Caiaphas, who was the high priest at the time of Jesus' Passion. From the seat of Moses, Caiaphas spoke prophetically on behalf of God in proclaiming Jesus' death:

> But one of them, named Caiphas, being the high priest that year, said to them: You know nothing. Neither do you consider that it is expedient for you that one man should die for the people, and that the whole nation perish not. And this he spoke not of himself: but being the high priest of that year, he prophesied that Jesus should die for the nation. And not only for the nation, but to gather together in one the children of God, that were dispersed.[6]

---

[6] Jn 11:49-52.

Caiaphas' proclamation was *binding* on the Sanhedrin because Scripture tells us: "From that day therefore they devised to put him to death" (Jn 11:53). Why does God reveal this? To demonstrate that He uses sinful men to teach authoritatively because of the office that they hold, and not because of their faithfulness or sanctity. Caiaphas did not speak of his own accord, but spoke on behalf of God Himself (see v. 51).

In Matthew 23:2-4, Jesus acknowledges that the scribes and Pharisees are the legitimate successors to the chair of Moses, and teach with his authority (which was true on the Old Testament side of the cross). Jesus also tells His disciples to observe "whatsoever" the scribes and Pharisees say (see v. 3). The Greek word for "whatsoever" (*panta hosa*) means "everything," which means Jesus regarded the Pharisees' authority as plenary and absolute.

But even though they have legitimate teaching authority, Jesus criticizes the scribes and Pharisees for their hypocritical behavior. They "bind" heavy burdens, but do not "loose" (move) them with their finger (see v. 4). Jesus goes on to say: "But woe to you scribes and Pharisees, hypocrites; because *you shut the kingdom of heaven* against men, for you yourselves do not enter in; and those that are going in, you suffer not to enter" (Mt 23:13).

In other words, Jesus recognizes the scribes and Pharisees' authority to "bind" and "loose," and to "shut" the kingdom of heaven against men (remember Eliakim's authority to "open" and "shut" in the kingdom of God). But Jesus says they are abusing their authority. They are exercising their authority with pride and contempt for their fellow man. They think they are better than everyone else because of their exalted position as teachers of the Law. Jesus goes on to indict them for their enlarged phylacteries, their places of honor at feasts and synagogues, and their basking in the title of "Rabbi" (Mt 23:5-7).

By giving Peter the keys and the authority to bind and loose, Jesus was annulling the old teaching authority of the Sanhedrin, and creating a new teaching authority, the Church. The one who sat on the "chair" of Peter would replace the one who sat on the "chair" (in Greek, *cathedra*) of Moses.[7] Just as the New Covenant would replace the Old, and the system of grace would replace the system of law, the apostles would replace the scribes and Pharisees as the official interpreters of the Word of God.[8]

Like Moses, Peter would have the authority to render the "judgment of God" (Ex 18:15). Like the Sanhedrin, Peter would be able to "shut the kingdom of heaven against men" who separate themselves from his teaching.[9] Like Eliakim, what Peter would "open, none shall shut."[10] Like Moses, Peter would be the official interpreter of God's Word.[11] Like Moses, who nourished his faithful with water from the rock, God would nourish the Church through the rock of Peter.[12] Like Joseph, Moses, and Eliakim, Peter would be second only to the King and would exercise his authority over all the people of the land.[13] Further, Jesus tells Peter that "whatsoever" he binds or looses on earth is bound or loosed in heaven (see Mt 16:19).

---

[7] When the pope invokes the charism of infallibility to protect his teachings on faith or morals, such teachings are considered *ex cathedra* (from the chair) teachings. Also, the principal church in a diocese is called a *cathedral* (meaning "the church containing the throne of the bishop").

[8] God always appointed an authority to interpret His Scriptures. Unlike what many "Bible" Christians contend, it would have been unthinkable (and biblically unprecedented) for God to give us Scriptures without also giving us an authority to interpret them.

[9] See Mt 23:13.

[10] See Is 22:22.

[11] For example, Peter makes a judgment on the proper interpretation of Paul's epistles. See 2 Pet 3:16.

[12] See Ex 17:6; 1 Cor 10:4.

[13] See Gen 41:43-44.

The Case for Papal Infallibility

The reciprocity between Peter's decisions on earth and God's decisions in heaven is nothing short of astounding. What Peter binds, heaven binds. What Peter looses, heaven looses. In the inspired Greek, heaven's reciprocal binding (*estai dedemenon*) and loosing (*estai lelumenon*) are in the passive voice. This could be translated as "shall be bound," or "shall having been bound." This means that heaven is *receiving* the binding or loosing from Peter, and ratifying Peter's decisions on earth. Just as God revealed to Peter a truth of salvation (Jesus is the Christ), God will now confirm Peter's teachings on salvation (about the same Jesus Christ).

Yet the future tense ("shall be bound") indicates that heaven's ratification of Peter's decisions has already occurred at the time Peter makes his decisions. The Holy Spirit's unique use of the future tense with the passive voice to describe heaven's reciprocal binding and loosing underscores that Peter truly speaks for heaven, just as he did when he confessed the divinity of Christ. Peter's binding and loosing decisions are ordained by God. When Peter makes such a decision, God in effect says: "Consider it already done."

Note also that Jesus tells Peter "whatsoever" (in Greek, *ho ean*) he binds and looses is bound or loosed in heaven.[14] This is another incredible component of the authority Jesus confers upon Peter. By saying "whatsoever," Jesus gives Peter the freedom to decide what he will bind and loose (the subject matter, scope, and limitations). Since Peter articulated the revelation from God, Peter will also articulate the application of his divinely appointed authority. The Church has always understood Peter's binding and loosing authority to be limited to teachings on faith and morals, which we will discuss further later.

---

[14] See Mt 16:19. Jesus used a similar word for "whatsoever" to describe the Pharisees' old binding and loosing authority (see Mt 23:3).

Matthew 16:18-19 presents a clear and convincing case for papal infallibility. Why? *Because God cannot deceive us.* As Paul says in his letter to the Hebrews, "It is impossible for God to lie."[15] God means what He says. If Jesus promises that heaven will ratify Peter's decisions, then Peter's teachings *must be true*, for God cannot confirm error. Jesus could not make such a promise to Peter unless He was certain that Peter's teachings would be free of all error.

But since Peter is only a fallible human being, God *must* provide the mechanism by which Peter is protected from teaching error. This, of course, is the working of the Holy Spirit. As He did with giving Peter a divine revelation, God penetrates the mind of Peter to prevent him from issuing erroneous teachings. Just as God initiated the appointment of Peter as head of the Church through divine intervention, God will continue to intervene in Peter's life as Peter fulfills his divinely appointed role.

This is the meaning of infallibility — that God protects Peter and his successors from teaching error on matters relevant to our salvation. Whenever the pope definitively teaches a matter on faith and morals to be believed by the universal Church (either singularly or together with the world's bishops united to him), the teaching is free from error.[16] God prevents His Church from "going off the tracks." The Church's two-thousand-year history of consistent, dogmatic teaching in our confused and divided world bears witness to this truth.

---

[15] Heb 6:18; see also Tit 1:2.

[16] When the pope singularly issues a definitive teaching on faith and morals to be believed by the entire Church and intends the teaching to be infallible, it is an *ex cathedra* teaching. When the pope issues a definitive teaching on faith and morals through a council (a gathering of the world's bishops in union with the pope), it is a *conciliar* teaching. The Catholic Church has invoked twenty-one ecumenical councils in her two-thousand year history.

God's gift of papal infallibility is an incredible blessing to the Church, second only to the seven sacraments instituted by Jesus Christ. But we should expect nothing less from our loving and merciful Father. Since He desires to give all men salvation,[17] God is bound by His justice to provide us a mechanism for understanding the truths of salvation. Otherwise, God's desire would be inconsistent with His action. This is impossible. God thus makes provisions (an infallible Church) to effect His desire (our salvation). While respecting our free will, God does not leave our salvation to chance, especially when Satan seeks to destroy us.

Isaiah prophesied about the infallibility of the Church when he wrote: "And a path and a way shall be there, and it shall be called the holy way: the unclean shall not pass over it, and this shall be unto you a straight way, so that fools shall not err therein."[18] The early Church was called "the way," which is the subject of Isaiah's prophecy.[19] "Fools will not err" in the Church only if God protects them from erring.

Before Jesus ascends into heaven, He assures Peter and the apostles that they will be divinely guided and protected by the Holy Spirit: "And I will ask the Father, and he shall give you another Paraclete, that he may abide with you for ever" (Jn 14:16). Jesus sends the Spirit to not only comfort the apostles, but to *teach* them all things regarding the deposit of faith: "But the Counselor, the Holy Spirit, whom the Father will send in my name, he will teach you all things, and bring to your remembrance all that I have said to you."[20] Jesus makes it clear that the Spirit will speak through the apostles: "For it is not you who

---

[17] See 1 Tim 2:4; 2 Pt 3:9; Mt 18:14; Ezech 18:23, 32 (Ezek in RSV-CE); Ecclesiasticus 15:11-12 (Sirach in RSV-CE).

[18] Is 35:8; see also Is 54:13-17.

[19] See Acts 9:2; 18:25, 26; 19:9; 22:4; 24:14, 22.

[20] Jn 14:26 (RSV-CE).

speak, but the Spirit of your Father speaking through you."[21] Again, Jesus says:

> I have yet many things to say to you: but you cannot bear them now. But when he, the Spirit of truth, is come, he will teach you all truth. For he shall not speak of himself; but what things soever he shall hear, he shall speak; and the things that are to come, he shall shew you.[22]

The Holy Spirit abides with Peter and the apostles and teaches them all truth. This empowers Peter and the apostles to hand this truth on to the Church, without the possibility of error. Peter will lead these efforts as the rock of the Church and the keeper of the keys. What Peter teaches on earth will be confirmed in heaven.

John professes the apostles' teaching authority when he says: "We are of God. He that knoweth God, heareth us. He that is not of God, heareth us not. By this we know the spirit of truth, and the spirit of error."[23] John says that we know the difference between truth and error by listening to those in authority, *not by reading the Bible*.

Of course, if listening to fallible men is the way God wants us to know truth from error, God must endow His chosen leaders with the ability to teach without error. The apostles recognize that they are collaborating with the Holy Spirit when they issue their apostolic letter to the Church after the Council of Jerusalem (more on this later): "For it has seemed good to the Holy Spirit and to us to lay upon you no greater burden than these necessary things" (Acts 15:28; RSV-CE).

In his letter to the Ephesians, Paul gives us some incredible insights into his understanding of the Church:

---

[21] Mt 10:20 (RSV-CE); see also Lk 12:12.
[22] Jn 16:12-13.
[23] 1 Jn 4:6.

And to enlighten all men, that they may see what is the dispensation of the mystery which hath been hidden from eternity in God, who created all things: That the manifold wisdom of God may be made known to the principalities and powers in heavenly places through the church, according to the eternal purpose, which he made, in Christ Jesus our Lord."[24]

Paul says that the "manifold wisdom of God" is "made known . . . through the church" (v. 10). Even the angels, who are intellectually superior to the Church's fallible human leaders, learn of God's wisdom through the infallible Church. Paul calls this the mystery that was hidden from eternity in God, and now revealed to all men (see v. 9).

Paul continues to explain that God works through the Church to accomplish His ends more effectively than the Church's leaders could ever desire or understand: "Now to him who is able to do all things more abundantly than we desire or understand, according to the power that worketh in us; to him be glory in the church, and in Christ Jesus unto all generations, world without end. Amen."[25]

Notice also that Paul says that Christ's Church exists in *all generations*. Only the Catholic Church satisfies that criterion. Paul finishes his discussion on the Church by describing her as "not having spot or wrinkle, or any such thing; but that it should be holy, and without blemish" (Eph 5:27). The Church cannot be without blemish if she is capable of teaching error.

While they may not be aware of it, non-Catholic Christians accept many infallible decisions of the popes of the Catholic Church. For example, all Christians generally accept the Church's infallible teachings on the Trinity and Christology, which were formulated by popes and councils during the first few centuries after

---

[24] Eph 3:9-11.
[25] Eph 3:20-21

Christ's ascension. Our understanding of the coequal substance of the three divine persons, the interior relationships within the Godhead, and the two wills and natures of Christ have all been defined by the Catholic Church.

The Catholic Church also infallibly defined the canon of Scripture. The canon of Scripture is the list of books that belong in the Bible. For example, the New Testament's canon contains twenty-seven books that all Protestants accept as divinely inspired. The Church's determination of the canon at the end of the fourth century is one of the most compelling proofs of her infallibility. Let's look at this issue in more detail.

The Canon of Scripture

Protestants generally believe that all the saving truths of the Christian faith are found in the Bible alone. They consequently believe that nothing necessary for our salvation comes to us from outside the Bible. As we have mentioned, this view is called *sola Scriptura*. While most Protestant communities are based on this doctrine, the canon of Scripture strikes it a fatal blow. Why? Because knowing the canon of Scripture is a saving truth of the Christian faith *that comes to us from outside the Bible*.

Knowing the canon is necessary for our salvation because, if we didn't know it, heretical books could have been mixed up with inspired texts. We must remember that many books were floating around Judea during the first century of the Church, including fifty separate gospels. These books all claimed divine inspiration, as their authors sought to cash in on the new Christian religion. If these erroneous books would have been accepted as canonical, Christians would have been led into error. God's revelation would have been compromised, and our salvation jeopardized.

However, none of the books in the Bible tell us what the canon is. Of course, why would they, since none of the authors of the books ever intended on compiling their works into a single, comprehensive treatise on Christianity. The books were written over a period of time to address specific theological and disciplinary issues in various churches within different geographies. Moreover, Jesus did not reveal the Bible canon to His apostles. After Christ's ascension, the canon was the subject of three and a half centuries of intense debate. If Christ would have revealed the canon to His apostles, there would have been no debate.

Yet, Jesus knew that some of the apostles would write Scripture at the direction of the Holy Spirit after His ascension.[26] Jesus also knew that many others would falsely claim to be writing divinely inspired Scripture. Since Jesus didn't reveal the canon, and since this knowledge was necessary for our salvation, *Jesus must have established an authority that would guarantee the early Christians' ability to determine the canon after His ascension into heaven.*

This authority was the Holy Catholic Church. Under the direction of Pope Damasus, the 36th successor to Peter, the Church first determined the canon of Scripture at a regional council in Rome in A.D. 382. This decision was affirmed by later popes,[27] and elevated to a dogmatic decree in 1546 by the Council of Trent under Pope Paul III, the 219th successor to Peter. The Catholic Church is the verifiable link between Christ's ascension (A.D. 33) and the compilation of the Bible (A.D. 382).

Because the Bible canon is infallible (without error) and the Catholic Church determined it, *Christ endowed the Catholic Church with the authority to make infallible decisions.* Those who

---

[26] Only five of the original apostles wrote Scripture (Peter, Matthew, John, James, and Jude). This demonstrates that the Gospel was to be principally transmitted orally through the Church.

[27] For example, the canon of Scripture was affirmed at the regional councils of Hippo and Carthage in A.D. 393 and 397, respectively, under Pope Siricius, the thirty-seventh successor to Peter, and again at the council of Carthage in 419 A.D. under Pope Boniface, the forty-first successor to Peter.

are unwilling to acknowledge the Church's infallible decisions attempt to downplay the canon's significance. For example, some non-Catholics argue that the Bible canon is nothing more than a fallible collection of infallible books. Arguing the canon is fallible allows the non-Catholic to skirt the issue of why he doesn't follow the Church's other infallible teachings.

Of course, if the canon were fallible, then why should we believe that the books in the canon are themselves infallible? A fallible canon would mean that other books could be added to the canon, and that books currently in the canon could be removed. In other words, the Christian would be arguing that the book on which he bases his theology and entire Christian life may not be giving us the whole picture. This would also mean that we would have no objective basis for denying the canonicity of other religious writings, such as the Book of Mormon or the Koran.

A principle of logic is that an effect can never be greater than its cause.[28] This means that, if the canon of Scripture is infallible (which it must be), its determination had to come from an infallible source as well. Arguing the canon is fallible, paradoxically, undermines the reliability and exclusivity of the Bible, which is the sole foundation on which Protestant Christianity is based.

Non-Catholic Christians also attempt to downplay the Church's infallible determination of the canon by saying that the canon exists because God inspired the books in it. Thus, they claim that the canon cannot be separated from the books themselves. But this argument begs the question because it doesn't answer how we know what books are inspired to begin with. The argument erroneously merges "knowledge" with "existence."

Knowledge and existence are two separate things, because something can exist without our knowing about it. For example, the Trinity existed but we didn't know about it until the Catholic

---

[28] This is called the "principle of causality."

Church defined it for us. Thus, the issue is not whether the canon exists (it clearly does), but how we *know* what books should be in it. If the canon cannot be found in the inspired books, this necessarily means that the canon is *separate and distinct* from those books.

The Spirit who guided the Church to infallibly determine the canon of Scripture is the *same Spirit* who guides the Church to infallibly interpret the books in the canon. When Philip saw the Ethiopian eunuch reading Isaiah, he said: "Thinkest thou that thou understandest what thou readest?"[29] The eunuch responded: "And how can I, unless some man shew me?"[30] *Scripture itself teaches us that an outside authority must be its interpreter and custodian.* The Scriptures are not self-interpreting or self-authenticating.[31]

Peter, the first pope, also warns us: "Understanding this first, that no prophecy of scripture is made by private interpretation."[32] If Scripture is not a matter of private interpretation, it is a matter of the *public interpretation of the Church*. This is the One, Holy, Catholic and Apostolic Church, which Jesus builds on the rock of Peter and the foundation of the other apostles.

We recall that Paul commands us to obey both the oral and written traditions (see 2 Thess 2:14). Paul's instruction presupposes that there is a way to determine what the authentic apostolic traditions are, for Paul would not command us to do the impossible. How do we know which traditions we must obey? We "hear

---

[29] Acts 8:30.

[30] Acts 8:31.

[31] For example, God speaks directly to Samuel three times, but Samuel does not recognize His voice (1 Kings 3:1-9 [1 Sam in RSV-CE]). The Word of God is not self-attesting. Just as God collaborated with human beings to write the sacred texts, He also works with human beings in guiding us to properly interpret them.

[32] 2 Pet 1:20.

the church," as Jesus instructs us (see Mt 18:17). Just as the Catholic Church determined the written tradition, she determines the unwritten tradition as well.

The Limits of Infallibility

We should note that God's gift of infallibility to the Church is only a negative protection. The Holy Spirit does not inspire the pope to teach infallibly. He only protects the pope from teaching error on faith and morals when the pope manifestly invokes His protection. Since Peter is the rock of the Church, Peter's office must be immune from error. If the foundation is not secure, the Church would be at risk. If the foundation is secure, the gates of hell will not prevail, as Jesus promised (and He always keeps His promises). Popes have invoked the Holy Spirit's protection cautiously throughout the centuries, and generally only when it has been necessary to end speculation about a doctrine, or eliminate a heresy.

Note also that God does not protect the pope's private opinions from error, nor does He preserve the pope from acting immorally. God protects the pope's official teachings on the faith only when the pope intends to bind the entire Church to them. Thus, infallibility attaches only to the authentic teaching *office* of the pope and not to the individual man holding the office. This makes sense, since infallibility concerns the salvation of the Church as a whole. Obviously, the pope's private opinions or personal conduct does not affect our salvation (but may affect his own).

Protestants, who base their faith on the Bible alone, should have no problem with the truth that sinners can teach infallibly. That is because all the books in the Bible were written by sinners, and yet their writings are infallible. Just look at Peter. He denied Jesus three times and yet wrote two infallible encyclicals, (that is, letters — 1 Peter and 2 Peter). Moses was a murderer, and David was an adulterer and murderer. Yet, God made Moses the official interpreter of His Word, and inspired him to write the first five books of the Bible (called the "Pentateuch").

God also made David the king of His earthly kingdom and inspired him to write the beautiful Psalms. We have also seen how God used Caiaphas to orally issue an infallible declaration, even though he rejected Jesus. If God directed sinners to teach infallibly during the age of the early Church, God can do the same thing today. God inspires sinners to teach infallibly, just as He inspires sinners to become saints.

The Catholic Church has never claimed that her popes are perfect paragons of virtue, who always practice what they preach and never err in their private opinions or personal conduct. Any such criticisms, if they seek to undermine the papal office, are misguided. Popes are sinners like the rest of us. If not, they would be "impeccable" (infallibility does not concern impeccability). In fact, the Church's canon law (promulgated by the pope himself) directs us to raise our concerns or objections to the pope and the rest of the prelature if we believe something in their administration is amiss, so long as it is done with dignity and respect.[33]

Because the distinction between a pope's official teachings and his private opinions is so important to the life of the Church, God wanted to make sure we understood the distinction. This is why God revealed in Scripture two situations in which Peter was rebuked (by Jesus and Paul). These situations demonstrate that popes can err in their private opinions without undermining the authority of their teaching office. Let's examine these two occurrences.

---

[33] See Canon 212 §§ 2-3. While we have a canonical right and even a duty to raise our concerns to the Church hierarchy, we must do so with great caution and charity, out of respect for the Vicar of Christ.

Jesus Rebukes Peter

We have seen how Jesus first revealed to His apostles that He would have to suffer and die in Jerusalem right after promising to give Peter the keys: "From that time Jesus began to shew to his disciples, that he must go to Jerusalem, and suffer many things from the ancients and scribes and chief priests, and be put to death, and the third day rise again" (Mt 16:21). After Jesus explained His Messianic mission, we read the following: "And Peter taking him, began to rebuke him, saying: Lord, be it far from thee, this shall not be unto thee. Who turning, said to Peter: Go behind me, Satan, thou art a scandal unto me: because thou savourest not the things that are of God, but the things that are of men."[34]

Because Jesus tells Peter, in effect, "Begone, Satan," many non-Catholics argue that Peter was prone to error and thus could not have been invested with the charism of infallibility. This argument demonstrates a significant misunderstanding of infallibility. When Peter told the Lord that "this shall not happen to you," he obviously wasn't issuing a binding teaching on the Church. He was expressing his loving concern for Jesus and His well-being. What friend wouldn't do the same?

In fact, at this time, Peter did not have any official teaching authority because he was not yet the head of the Church. Jesus' promises to Peter in Matthew 16:18-19 are all in the future tense, meaning that Peter would not take his office until Christ ascended into heaven. Only at that point would the Church need a chief steward. We have already explained that a pope's private opinions do not come within the domain of infallibility.

Moreover, even though Peter's statement is a private opinion and not an official teaching, it is really not fair to criticize Peter's statement. Remember, this was the first time that Jesus told His

---

[34] Mt 16:22-23

apostles about His future death and resurrection. Since this was the first time that Jesus revealed the Father's plan to His apostles, Peter had no prior knowledge of it and was taken by complete surprise. Further, since Jesus had not yet explained *why* He had to suffer and die, Peter and the rest of the apostles obviously did not have a complete understanding of it. Thus, Peter's statement was nothing more than a quick and compassionate reaction to Jesus' shocking revelation, which the other apostles evidently did not express in the same way.

Of course, Jesus' rebuke of Peter did not usurp the authority Jesus would ultimately confer upon him. Jesus says nothing about removing the keys that He promised to give Peter, or stripping Peter of his divine duties. Such a divestiture would also not make any sense in light of other Gospel texts where Jesus, at a later time, charges Peter to shepherd the Church and strengthen the other apostles (more on this later).[35] The fact that Peter went on to lead the early Church and write two infallible encyclicals that explain the Father's plan in Christ further undermines the argument against Peter's authority. While Peter was a temporary stumbling block for Christ, he, as the rock of the Church, would be a permanent stumbling block for Satan.

Why was Jesus so severe with Peter? Because Jesus wanted to declare that He would accomplish the Father's plan at all costs. Jesus uses similar language in Matthew 4:10, when He rebuked Satan during His temptations in the desert.[36] By using a similar rebuke with Peter, Jesus was affirming to Satan that no one, not even the future leader of His Church, would be able to frustrate God's plan. In obedience to the Father and love for humanity,

---

[35] See Lk 22:31-32 and Jn 21:15-17.

[36] In Greek, "*hupage opiso mou satana.*" See also Mk 8:33. The Bible often uses the Greek word *satana* to mean "adversary," which is the context in which Jesus uses the word in Matthew 4:10. Jesus was not calling Peter "evil." Jesus was telling Peter that his statement was "adversarial" to God's plan.

Jesus was going to the cross for the sins of the world, and no one or nothing was going to stop Him.

Jesus was also severe with Peter because He wanted Peter to comprehend the real meaning of Christian leadership: *self-sacrifice, even to the point of death.* Peter's response indicates that he did not understand the significance of Jesus' pending suffering and death. Peter may also have had some mistaken notions about the royal authority Jesus had just promised to give him. Jesus was now going to set Peter straight. Immediately after getting Peter's attention with the stinging rebuke, Jesus says: "If any man will come after me, let him deny himself, and take up his cross, and follow me. For he that will save his life, shall lose it: and he that shall lose his life for my sake, shall find it."[37]

Rather than explaining the theology of the atonement, Jesus tells Peter and the other apostles that true discipleship, and ultimately eternal life, requires laying one's life down in sacrifice. Anything less than that "are the things of men, not God."[38] Unlike the Pharisees, who wielded their authority over God's people, Peter and the apostles would be servants. Jesus says many times: "And behold, they are last that shall be first; and they are first that shall be last."[39] If Peter was going to lead the Church as the Vicar of Christ, he would have to follow in His Master's footsteps.

Jesus would later predict Peter's eventual martyrdom,[40] which Peter himself writes about[41] and eventually embraced. In fact, every successor of Peter during the first centuries of the Church was also brutally martyred. Ascending to the throne of Peter meant certain death. This holy witness of service and self-sacrifice has led Catholics to call the pope "the servant of the servants of God."

---

[37] Mt 16:24-25.

[38] See Mt 16:23.

[39] Lk13:30; see also Mt 19:30; 20:16; 23:11-12; Mk 9:34; 10:31, 43-45.

[40] See Jn 13:36; 21:18.

[41] See 2 Pet 1:14.

Jesus' rebuke of Peter did not diminish Peter's authority; *it clarified the real meaning of it.*

Paul Rebukes Peter

Many opponents of the papacy also point to Paul's letter to the Galatians, where Paul rebukes Peter for separating himself from the Gentiles during meals. This is another example where Peter is rebuked for his personal conduct, and not his teaching authority. The passage is found in Galatians 2:11-14:

> But when Cephas came to Antioch I opposed him to his face, because he stood condemned. For before certain men came from James, he ate with the Gentiles; but when they came he drew back and separated himself, fearing the circumcision party. And with him the rest of the Jews acted insincerely, so that even Barnabas was carried away by their insincerity. But when I saw that they were not straightforward about the truth of the gospel, I said to Cephas before them all, "If you, though a Jew, live like a Gentile and not like a Jew, how can you compel the Gentiles to live like Jews?"[42]

Non-Catholics who attack the papacy make way too much out of this passage as well. The fact that God inspired Paul to write about this occurrence actually highlights Peter's prominence in the early Church. After all, as we will discuss later, Peter was the first to declare that the Gentiles were full members of the New Covenant.[43] Peter was also the first to baptize the Gentiles.[44] Paul even refers to Peter as "Cephas," which underscores Peter's supe-

---

[42] RSV-CE.
[43] See Acts 10:45-48; 11:1; 15:7-11.
[44] See Acts 10:47-48.

riority over Paul and the magnitude of Paul's rebuke. Nevertheless, Paul evidently felt that Peter was not living up to his infallible teaching. The Greek word for "acted insincerely" in verse 13 (*hupokrisei*) indicates that Paul believed Peter was acting hypocritically (that is, he was violating his own rule).

Since Paul was an apostle to the Gentiles, he was sensitive to the manner in which they were being evangelized. Paul viewed Peter's decision to separate from them during meals as an obstacle to their evangelization. Since Peter was the head of the Church, the Gentiles would have naturally (and mistakenly) looked to Peter's conduct as representative of the Church's teaching. Peter's conduct was under the microscope, and his decision to separate from them would have sent the Gentiles a mixed message. Were they really equal members of the Church? Paul, in fulfilling his God-given mission to the Gentiles, believed he had to confront Peter about his behavior.

Many people are too quick to conclude that Peter sinned by separating himself from the Gentiles. Peter's conduct could be perceived as perfectly reasonable. From Peter's perspective, the Gentiles should have known that they were full-fledged members of the New Covenant. Peter had preached the Gospel to them and had baptized them. Peter definitively declared that they too were saved by Jesus. As we will examine later, Peter also definitively taught that the Gentiles did not have to submit to the Jews' long-standing practice of circumcision (see Acts 15:7-11).

The Jews, on the other hand, had always viewed themselves as God's favored people and superior to the Gentiles. They had been given the "oracles of God."[45] If Peter were viewed as giving the Gentiles preferential treatment (for example, eating with them), this could have been offensive to the Jews. In fact, it *was* offensive

---

[45] See Rom 3:2.

to them. The Jews criticized Peter by asking him: "Why did you go to uncircumcised men and eat with them?"[46]

Since Peter's conduct troubled the Jews, and Peter had a special mission to convert them (as Paul did with the Gentiles), Peter made a pastoral decision to eat with the Jews and not with the Gentiles. Peter wanted to eliminate any obstacles to the Jews' conversion, and viewed his decision as for the good of the Church. Peter was not rendering an official and binding decision on whom a Christian should eat with; he was trying to maintain harmony in the Church by making the best out of a difficult situation.

Peter could have responded harshly to Paul's rebuke by accusing Paul of hypocrisy (*hupokrisei*) himself. Paul, on several occasions, also attempted to accommodate the Jews, in much more brazen ways than Peter did. For example, Paul had bishop Timothy circumcised "because of the Jews who were in those places" (Acts 16:3). This was in direct contravention of Paul's teachings that circumcision "avails nothing."[47]

Paul also underwent the Mosaic law of purification.[48] This contravened Paul's perennial teaching that no one is justified by "works of the law."[49] Yet Paul engaged in these Jewish practices to reach out to his former brethren so that he would have a chance to preach the Gospel to them. Paul's actions were simply for the sake of pastoral care. He probably should have known that Peter's actions had the same objective.

Peter Teaches Paul

In his letter to the Galatians, Paul also reveals that he spent fifteen days with Peter, his superior, *to learn about the Christian faith.*

---

[46] Acts 11:3 (RSV-CE).
[47] See Gal 5:2, 6.
[48] See Acts 21:24, 26.
[49] See, for example, Rom 3:20, 28; Gal 2:16.

Galatians 1:18-19 says: "Then after three years I went up to Jerusalem to visit Cephas, and remained with him fifteen days. But I saw none of the other apostles except James the Lord's brother."[50]

This is another insightful passage that highlights Peter's supremacy in the early Church. In describing his trip to Jerusalem, Paul records that he saw both Peter and James. The English translation makes it fairly clear that the purpose of Paul's trip to Jerusalem was to see Peter, and not James. The inspired Greek language makes this even clearer, since Paul uses very different verbs to describe how he "saw" Peter versus how he "saw" James.

Paul says that he went "to visit" (*historesai*) Peter, but that he only "saw" (*eidon*) James. This is a significant difference. *Eidon* means "to see," but *historesai* means much more. When I studied the ancient legal systems in law school, I learned that a *histor* was a cross-examiner in the courts of Greece. The *histor* would ask a witness questions for purposes of obtaining evidence in a dispute. After weighing all of the evidence that he obtained through his cross-examination, the *histor* would resolve the dispute by rendering the final judgment.

The Greek verb *historesai* comes from its related noun *histor* and means "to examine." When Paul uses this verb to describe how he went "to visit" Peter, Paul means that he went to examine Peter *to obtain knowledge from him*. "To visit Peter" (*historesai Petron*) means to get information from Peter. Paul acted as the *histor*, and Peter as the witness. Peter was indeed the witness to Jesus' resurrection, and he was the rock of the Church. Paul recognizes the same by referring to Peter as "Cephas" elsewhere in the letter (see Gal 2:14). If Paul was to faithfully fulfill his ministry, he would have to learn what Peter knew and teach what Peter taught. Paul made sure of this by questioning Peter for fifteen days.

---

[50] RSV-CE.

We can only speculate about what Peter taught Paul during this two-week period. Two weeks is an incredible amount of time for any two people to meet, much less two important leaders of the infant Catholic Church. We can be sure that Peter answered Paul's questions, and that Paul received an extensive catechesis from Peter during this time. Peter and Paul would have also celebrated the Eucharist together. Why does God inspire Paul to record his visit with Peter? To honor Peter as the Vicar of Christ, and demonstrate Paul's submission to his authority.

What about James? Paul says that he only saw James, but did not inquire anything of him. In fact, James was the bishop of Jerusalem, and yet Paul chose to spend fifteen days in Jerusalem with Peter, not James. Since James was the bishop of Jerusalem, this would have been a very disrespectful thing for Paul to do, unless Peter had authority over James. Although James held the seat of authority in Jerusalem, Peter held the seat of authority over the universal Church, and Paul chose to get his information from Peter, not James. Again, this demonstrates Peter's authority over the other apostles.

Didn't Jesus Also Give the Other Apostles the Authority to Bind and Loose?

Yes. Jesus does this by describing a situation where an unrepentant sinner is brought to a local church for rebuke. We see this in Matthew 18:15-18:

> If your brother sins against you, go and tell him his fault, between you and him alone. If he listens to you, you have gained your brother. But if he does not listen, take one or two others along with you, that every word may be confirmed by the evidence of two or three witnesses. If he refuses to listen to them, tell it to the church; and if he refuses to listen even to the church, let him be to you as

a Gentile and a tax collector. Truly, I say to you, whatever you bind on earth shall be bound in heaven, and whatever you loose on earth shall be loosed in heaven.[51]

It is clear that Jesus confers this authority upon the other apostles.[52] The word "you" (in Greek, *humin*) is plural (see vv. 18-19). The "binding" (*deseste*) and "loosing" (*lusete*) are also in the plural (see v. 18). Non-Catholics try to marginalize Peter's authority over the Church by arguing that the apostles had the same authority as Peter. Ironically, these are generally the same people who argue that the Church has no divine authority at all. As we will see, the binding and loosing authority that Jesus gives Peter is different from the authority that He gives the rest of the apostles.

First, we recall that Jesus mentions "binding and loosing" and the "Church" only twice in the entire New Testament. In each instance, the terms are inexorably connected (see Mt 16:18-19 and Mt 18:17-18). As we see in these passages, "binding and loosing" are functions of the "Church," and thus they cannot be understood outside the context of the Church.

With that said, we know that Peter *alone* is the rock of the Church, and Peter *alone* was given the keys to the kingdom of heaven (the Church). Because binding and loosing is a power of the keys which Peter *alone* holds, the apostles' authority to bind and loose is *dependent upon the authority of Peter*. This is why Jesus does not mention "keys" in Matthew 18:17-18. Where the authority will reside is no longer in question. The apostles already under-

---

[51] RSV-CE.

[52] In Mt 18:1, it says Jesus began this dialogue with "the disciples" (not "the apostles"). Because Matthew does not say "apostles," some non-Catholics erroneously conclude that Jesus conferred the authority to bind and loose on all Christians. But Matthew refers to the twelve apostles as "the disciples." For example, see Mt 10:1 and 26:20 where the twelve apostles are called the "twelve disciples." See also Mt 26:17-19. As in these cases, Matthew was referring to the apostles in Mt 18:15-18.

stand that Christ will give His keys to Peter, which symbolize the binding and loosing authority that Peter individually possesses. Jesus' point in Matthew 18:17-18 is to tell the apostles that *they too* will share in Peter's authority as they run their local churches, so long as they share the rock foundation of Peter.

Thus, in Matthew 16:19, Jesus gives Peter the *singular* authority to bind and loose. In Matthew 18:18, Jesus gives the apostles the *collegial* authority to bind and loose. Jesus confers the authority upon Peter *personally*, and upon the apostles *in common*. Jesus (re)names Peter, but He does not mention the names of the other apostles. The college of apostles (and later bishops and cardinals) is an authoritative body only to the extent the members are in union with the rock of Peter.

While Peter can bind and loose at his own will and pleasure, the other apostles can bind and loose only with Peter's consent. This is reflected by the teachings and disciplines Peter gives the entire Church, and the apostles' conformity to them. Just as the Sanhedrin exercised binding and loosing authority in union with the one who sat on the chair of Moses, the bishops exercise their authority in union with Peter.

Why did Jesus give this authority to the other apostles? To ensure the unity and integrity of the faith as the Church expanded throughout the world. Jesus envisioned a universal (or "catholic") Church when He commanded His apostles to "teach all nations."[53] While this would require a chief shepherd (Peter) over the universal Church, it would also require additional shepherds over the local churches. After all, as the Church grew, Peter would not be able to rule on every single situation that cropped up around the world. Instead, Peter and his successors would appoint bishops to rule and govern particular geographical areas (we will discuss apostolic succession in greater detail later). These areas

---

[53] See Mt 28:19.

would eventually become known as "dioceses." The bishops would share in Peter's authority so long as they remained faithful to his teachings.

This is confirmed by the hypothetical that Jesus poses as He confers the authority upon the apostles. As we have read, Jesus describes the apostles' authority in the context of rebuking a sinner who is a local member of the community. If the sinner obstinately perseveres in his sin by not listening to the church, he is to be treated as a "heathen and publican" (Mt 18:17). A heathen was someone outside of God's covenant family. A publican, or tax collector, was also separated from the religious community because his job defiled him. In other words, Jesus authorizes the apostles to excommunicate the sinner from the local ecclesial community until he repents of his sin.[54]

Even though this is a local situation, the action taken by the apostles is considered taken by *the entire Church*. Why? Because the Church is *one* in doctrine and morals. If a person refuses to obey the local church's teaching, he sins against the whole Church. Christ endowed the Church with *one* faith, just as there is one Lord and one baptism.[55] Thus, the apostles will bind the universal truths of the Church at the local level. Jesus assumes this unity in Matthew 18:17-18 by referring to the Church as *ecclesia* (singular), without specifying the particular geographical location of the excommunication. Jesus can assume this unity because He prays to the Father for it, and His prayers are always answered.[56]

Because Peter holds the keys to the universal Church, any transgression of her teachings or discipline triggers the authority of

---

[54] For example, Paul recommends the excommunication of a fornicator in the local church of Corinth, which carries the full force of the Church universal (see 1 Cor 5:5). Paul also tells Timothy that he has excommunicated Hymenaeus and Alexander for disobedience (1 Tim 1:20).

[55] See Eph 4:5.

[56] See Jn 17:20-23.

the keys, *no matter where it occurs*. To ensure the purity of doctrine and the unity of the Church, Christ enables Peter to act through his designees, just as Christ acts through Peter. Peter's authority defends and confirms the authority of the other apostles. Jesus' delegation of this authority to the apostles ensures that "they all may be one" (Jn 17:21).

Many Catholics point out that Peter is given the binding and loosing authority in connection with declaring a theological truth (Jesus is the Christ). The other apostles are given the authority in connection with rendering a disciplinary action (excommunicating a sinner). Peter's declaration that Jesus is the Christ is a *matter of faith*. The apostles' disciplinary action is a *matter of morals*. This demonstrates that the Church's authority to bind and loose is exercised in the realm of faith and morals.

However, we cannot limit the apostles' binding and loosing authority to matters of morals, just like we cannot limit Peter's authority to matters of faith. In Matthew 18:15-18, Jesus doesn't specify whether the sin was against faith or morals, which means Jesus didn't circumscribe the apostles' authority to moral issues only. The sinner's offense could have very well been against the doctrine of the Church (for example, by spreading a heresy), and not against any explicit moral teaching of the Church.

In fact, there is a *faith* dimension in Matthew 18, and there is a *moral* dimension in Matthew 16. That is, everyone has a moral obligation to submit to Peter's teaching that Jesus is the Christ and Son of God. Further, everyone must have faith in the authentic disciplinary decisions of the Church (which come from the power of the keys and are ultimately rooted in questions of faith or morals). Thus, the passages in Matthew 16 and 18 should not be distinguished on the basis of faith versus morals, but on the basis of universal Church (see Mt 16:19) versus local church (see Mt 18:18).

Matthew 18:15-18 poses significant problems for "Bible" Christians. When there is a dispute among Christians, Jesus says: "Tell . . . the Church" (v. 17). Jesus does not say "tell the faithful," or "read him the Bible." What Church? Where does the Lutheran take his Methodist brother for correction? Where does the Episcopalian take his Pentecostal sister for reproof? In order for Jesus' instructions to be properly implemented, there must be a single, visible entity with authority, not a group of competing factions and splintering sects. This is demonstrated by Jesus' use of the word *ecclesia*. This is the city of God, built on the mountain of Peter, which cannot be hid.[57] The Church, and not the Bible, is the final authority on matters of the Christian faith.

As we have seen, Jesus' appointment of fallible leaders who had access to God's infallible decrees was nothing new to the Jews. God had appointed Moses and the Levitical priests over the people of Israel, to whom the Sanhedrin of Jesus' time traced their authority. Moses and his priests exercised divine judgments in God's holy name, and whoever disobeyed their infallible judgments would die. Deuteronomy 17:9-13 says:

> And coming to the Levitical priests, and to the judge who is in office in those days, you shall consult them, and they shall declare to you the decision. Then you shall do according to what they declare to you from that place which the LORD will choose; and you shall be careful to do according to all that they direct you; according to the instructions which they give you, and according to the decision which they pronounce to you, you shall do; you shall not turn aside from the verdict which they declare to you, either to the right hand or to the left. The man who acts presumptuously, by not obeying the priest who

---

[57] See Mt 5:14.

stands to minister there before the LORD your God, or the judge, that man shall die; so you shall purge the evil from Israel. And all the people shall hear, and fear, and not act presumptuously again.[58]

In the book of Numbers, we read about a man named Korah who, along with two hundred fifty of his followers, rose up against Moses and his priests (see Num 16). Korah sought the priesthood for himself, and he acted to usurp Moses and Aaron's divine authority (see Num 16:10). Since God cannot lie, He made good on the promise He made in Deuteronomy 17:12. As a consequence of their rebellion against His chosen leaders, God destroyed Korah and his followers by causing the earth to swallow them alive (see Num 16:33).

How is Korah's Old Testament rebellion relevant to Christians? The Apostle Jude warns the Church not to "perish in Korah's rebellion" (Jude 11; RSV-CE). One must ask this important question: Why would God inspire Jude to warn the faithful not to rebel as Korah did if there were no hierarchy in the Church to obey? How can we rebel like Korah if the Bible is our only authority? Jude's warning makes no sense unless God has appointed leaders in the Church who have divine authority, just as He did with Moses and the Levitical priests.

In his letter to the Hebrews, Paul exhorts the faithful to obey Church leaders who are caretakers of our souls: "Obey your prelates, and be subject to them. For they watch as being to render an account of your souls; that they may do this with joy, and not with grief. For this is not expedient for you" (Heb 13:17). If Christianity is just about "Jesus, the Bible, and me," God's exhortation to obey His chosen leaders would not make any sense.

---

[58] RSV-CE.

The Authority to Bind and Loose
Includes Forgiving Sins

The power of the keys gives Peter the authority to pronounce doctrinal judgments and make disciplinary decisions in the voice of Jesus Christ. But the keys also give Peter, and the apostles in union with him, the authority to forgive (loose) and retain (bind) sins. Sin, which came from Adam, leads to death.[59] Forgiveness of sin, which comes from the second Adam, Jesus Christ, leads to eternal life.[60] Jesus' keys symbolize His supernatural authority over life and death, and He gives these keys to Peter.

When Jesus forgave sins during His earthly ministry, He emphasized that He was forgiving those sins *as a man*: "But that you may know that the *Son of man* hath power on earth to forgive sins."[61] When Jesus refers to Himself as "Son of man," He is emphasizing His humanity. When He refers to Himself as "Son of God," He is emphasizing His divinity. Just as God entrusted the power to forgive sins to Jesus as a man, Jesus entrusts His apostles to forgive sins as men. Hence, Matthew says that God has given the authority to forgive sins "*to men*" (Mt 9:8).

Jesus' conferral of priestly authority to forgive sins upon Peter and the apostles is one of the most explicit teachings in Scripture. We read about this event in chapter 20 of John's Gospel, where Jesus appears to His apostles after His resurrection:

Jesus said to them again, "Peace be with you. As the Father has sent me, even so I send you." And when he had said this, he breathed on them, and said to them, "Receive

---

[59] See Rom 5:12.
[60] See Rom 5:16-21.
[61] Mt 9:6; see also Mk 2:10; Lk 5:24.

the Holy Spirit. If you forgive the sins of any, they are forgiven; if you retain the sins of any, they are retained."[62]

The way Jesus describes this authority demonstrates that it is part of "binding and loosing," which comes from the keys. Jesus could have alternatively said, "Whose sins you loose are loosed, and whose sins you bind are bound." In Jewish rabbinic terminology, "forgiving" is equated with loosing, permitting, opening, or absolving; "retaining" is equated with binding, forbidding, shutting, or condemning. Whatever terms we use, the apostles' supernatural authority over life (if the sin is forgiven) and death (if the sin is retained) is clear.

There are some other interesting parallels between John 20:23 and Matthew 16:19; 18:18. For example, Jesus says *"whose" sins you forgive or retain*. This corresponds to Jesus' statement *"whatever" you bind or loose*, in Matthew 16:19; 18:18. Peter and the apostles will have the prerogative to decide who will be granted God's forgiveness, which they will charitably exercise. Jesus also sets no limits to their ability to forgive sins. No matter how grave the sinner and how evil the sins, the apostles can loose them in the name of Christ. It is also obvious that a sinner would have to orally confess his sins to the apostles in order for them to exercise their authority.

There is also a definite correspondence between heaven and earth in John 20:23, just as there is in Matthew 16:19; 18:18. As in the verses from Matthew's Gospel, the first clause regards the action of the apostles on earth (whoever's sins you forgive or retain / whatsoever you bind or loose). The second clause regards the

---

[62] Jn 20:21-23(RSV-CE). This is the biblical basis for the Church's sacrament of penance (also called confession or reconciliation). Jesus Christ instituted seven sacraments to be celebrated by His Holy Catholic Church: baptism, penance, the Eucharist, confirmation, holy matrimony, holy orders, and anointing of the Sick.

action of God in heaven (they are forgiven or retained / they are bound or loosed). Jesus does not say: "Whoever's sins I forgive through you." Heaven receives the forgiving (loosing) or retaining (binding) directly from the apostles, and confirms them in eternity.

Jesus makes this clear in John 20 when He says: "As the Father has sent me, even so I send you" (v. 21). Just as the Father sent Jesus to forgive sins, Jesus now sends the apostles to forgive sins. Jesus also makes it clear that He is the source of the authority when He tells the apostles "*I* send you" (v. 21), just as He tells Peter "*I* will build my church" and "*I* will give to [you] the keys of the kingdom of heaven" (Mt 16:18, 19).

In addition, we see the explicit presence of the Holy Spirit in John 20:22, right before Christ delegates the binding and loosing authority in verse 23. This parallels Jesus' delegation of authority to Peter. In Matthew's Gospel, the Father gives the Holy Spirit to Peter, who is empowered to make an infallible declaration. In John's Gospel, Jesus gives the Holy Spirit to the apostles, who are empowered to forgive sins. In both cases, God reveals to the apostles the presence of the Holy Spirit *immediately before* He confers His authority upon them. This confirms for them that their authority is truly divine, and will help bring about the kingdom of heaven. We see the same thing with the Old Testament figures of Joseph and Moses, where God first gives them a divine revelation and then confers upon them divine authority.

Non-Catholics have trouble with John 20:21-23. Because they deny the sacramental priesthood, they must argue that Christ is not really conferring the priestly authority to forgive sins upon the apostles. They say the same thing that the scribes and Pharisees did about Jesus: "Who can forgive sins, but God only?"[63] Instead, they argue that Jesus is simply telling the apostles to forgive one

---

[63] Mk 2:7; Lk 5:21.

another. This, of course, denies the plain meaning of the text, as well as all of the biblical precedents where God gives His chosen leaders divine authority over His covenant people.

There is also no exegetical basis for the argument. When Jesus tells His disciples to forgive one another, He always focuses on the *forgiver's* salvation, not the salvation of the person being forgiven (as He does in John 20:23). For example, Jesus says: "For if you will forgive men their offences, your heavenly Father will forgive you also your offences. But if you will not forgive men, neither will your Father forgive you your offences."[64] Jesus also says, "Forgive, and you shall be forgiven" (Lk 6:37). In the Our Father, Jesus tells us to pray, "And forgive us our debts, as we also forgive our debtors."[65]

Jesus' focus in John 20:23 is quite different. Jesus says nothing about the effect that the apostles' act of forgiving will have on themselves. He is solely addressing the effect that it will have on the person being forgiven. Jesus does not say, "If you forgive someone's sins, you are forgiven as well." Jesus says, "If you forgive someone's sins, *they are forgiven*." Jesus makes a clear distinction between the forgiver's forgiveness and the penitent's forgiveness. This is also why the efficacy of the Church's sacraments does not depend upon the holiness of the priest who is celebrating them. His authority exists independently of his sanctity (or lack of it).

Non-Catholics also argue that Jesus is simply giving Christians the power to confront a sinner and declare to him his sins. But this is not what the text says. Jesus does not say, "Whose sins you declare, they are declared." Moreover, Jesus is in the Upper Room addressing His apostles only, so the passage is not about all Christian believers. This argument would also reduce the Church's moral code to the subjective judgment of her members, since it denies that any central authority has the final word. This is incon-

[64] Mt 6:14-15; see also Mt 18:35; Mk 11:25-26.
[65] Mt 6:12; see also Lk 11:4.

sistent with Jesus' command in Matthew 18:17 to take the sinner "to the church" for correction and reproof as a last resort. Such a relativistic view of morality, unfortunately, is the effect of "Bible-only" Christianity.

What Is "Retaining" Sin?

Another significant problem with the non-Catholic position is that it does not address the apostles' authority to "retain" sins. What does this mean? When Jesus gave the apostles the authority to forgive sins, He also gave them the authority to evaluate the spiritual condition of the penitent as they heard the confession. If, in the apostles' estimation, the penitent should be required to do penance in reparation for his sins (prayers, works of mercy), the apostles could *retain* the sins (withhold forgiveness) until the penance was performed. In other words, the apostles would *bind* the penitent to works of penance before they *loosed* the sins from his soul. Forgiving and retaining sins, while explicitly scriptural, has no place in Protestant theology.

The power to retain sin is extremely significant because it means the apostles not only have the authority to retain (bind) for-giveness, but also *to remove (loose) the temporal punishments due to sin*.[66] Because God is perfectly merciful, He sent His Son, Jesus, to save us from the eternal punishment due to our sins. But this does not mean that we now have a license to sin. Because God is perfectly just, He requires us to confess our sins and make repa-ration for them as members of Christ's body.[67] This reparation

---

[66] If a person commits a mortal sin, he would incur eternal punishment for that sin if he died without repenting of it. Only Christ can remove the eternal punishment for our sins. Mortal sin requires three elements: (1) grave matter, (2) knowledge with sufficient reflection, and (3) full consent of the will. If the sin does not meet these requirements, it is a venial sin and carries temporal punish-ments only. See 1 Jn 5:16-17.

[67] See 1 Jn 1:9.

removes the temporal punishment that we incurred in God's eyes for the sin we committed. For example, when David committed adultery with Bathsheba, God forgave David's sin, but punished David by taking the life of his child.[68]

While Jesus' propitiatory sacrifice makes our forgiveness possible, He did not "pay the full penalty for our sins," as many non-Catholics argue. If He did, then no one would go to hell, because God would not require a double payment for the same sin. That would not only be unjust, but would be inconsistent with Jesus' pervasive teaching that many people will go to hell.[69] To avoid hell and enter into heaven, we must *both* confess our sins to receive forgiveness (by God's mercy) *and* make reparation for them to achieve purity of soul (by God's justice). The Church calls the removal of temporal punishment due to sin already forgiven an "indulgence."

Purgation After Death by Fire

In 1 Corinthians 3:12-17, Paul writes about how God purifies us with fire after we die to make satisfaction for any remaining temporal punishment due Him. Paul uses a string of metaphors regarding building a temple with good or bad materials to describe this process. God's judgment reveals three types of persons:

- He who built with only good materials receives a reward (see v. 14).
- He who built with good and bad materials will have to pass through fire along with his works; his bad works are burned up, but he is still saved (see v. 15).

---

[68] See 2 Kings 12:13-14 (2 Sam in RSV-CE).
[69] See, for example, Mt 5:22, 29-30; 10:28; 18:9; 23:15; Mk 9:42, 44, 46; Lk 12:5.

- He who built with only bad materials has destroyed God's temple, and God will destroy him (see v. 17).

The person who built with only good materials is saved, and the person who built with only bad materials is damned. Regarding the person who built with both good and bad materials, Paul says: "If any man's work burn, he shall suffer loss; but he himself shall be saved, yet so as by fire" (v. 15).

Paul's phrase "suffer loss" (in Greek, *zemiothesetai*), when used elsewhere in Scripture, always refers to punishment.[70] This means that the man who did both good and bad works during his life is punished after his death, *but is still saved*. This process of a post-death punishment that precedes salvation, while clearly biblical, is foreign to Protestant Christianity.

How is he punished? Paul says "yet so as by fire" (v. 15). The phrase "yet so" (in Greek, *houtos*) means "in the same manner." This means that the man is punished in the same manner in which his bad works were burned up — *by fire*. The man must pass through the same fire that burned up his bad works in order to be saved. When the man passes through the fire, he "suffers loss" (from the Greek, *zemioo*), which means he undergoes an expiation of temporal punishment before he is given the crown of salvation.[71] The Church calls this state of purification "purgatory."[72]

"*Whatever* you bind and loose" includes the power to remove sin *and its temporal consequences*. If the consequences are not removed during our lives, they will be expiated in the fires of

---

[70] See, for example, Ex 21:22 and Prov 17:26; 19:19; 21:11; 22:3 where the same word (in Hebrew, *anash*) means "punish" or "penalty."

[71] For other biblical references to this purgatorial fire, see 1 Pt 1:6-7; Jude 23; Apoc 3:18-19 (Rev in RSV-CE); Wis 3:5-6; Ecclesiasticus 2:5 (Sirach in RSV-CE); Prov 17:3; Dn 12:10; Mal 3:2-3; and Zach 13:8-9 (Zech in RSV-CE).

[72] For an in-depth, scriptural explanation of purgatory, please see my book *The Biblical Basis for the Catholic Faith* (Our Sunday Visitor), pp. 218-227.

purgatory. Just as Jesus' keys "of death and hell" released the souls from Hades, the keys also release souls from purgatory (by remitting the punishment that would send or keep them there).

CHAPTER FIVE

—◦◊◦—

Peter Is the Chief Shepherd of the Church

We have seen how Jesus shares His divine attributes with Peter and the apostles. Jesus is our High Priest, and the apostles are also priests.[1] Jesus is the foundation of the Church and so are the apostles.[2] Jesus is the rock of the Church, and Peter is as well.[3] Jesus has the keys to the kingdom, and He gives these keys to Peter.[4] Jesus binds and looses, and so does Peter.[5] This chapter focuses on another divine attribute that Jesus shares with Peter: Being the *shepherd* of the Church.

In John's Gospel, Jesus reveals that He is the Good Shepherd:

I am the good shepherd. The good shepherd lays down his life for the sheep. . . . I am the good shepherd; I know my own and my own know me, as the Father knows me and I know the Father; and I lay down my life for the sheep. And I have other sheep, that are not of this fold; I must bring them also, and they will heed my voice. So there shall be one flock, one shepherd.[6]

---

[1] See Heb 3:1; 4:14-15; 5:5, 10; 6:20; 7:26; 8:1; 9:11; 10:21 / Acts 14:22; 15:2; 22:30; 1 Tim 5:17, 19; Tit 1:5; James 5:14; Apoc 1:6; 5:10; 20:6 (Rev in RSV-CE).

[2] See Eph 2:20 / 1 Cor 3:11.

[3] See 1 Cor 10:4 / Mt 16:18.

[4] See Apoc 3:7 / Mt 16:19.

[5] See Apoc 3:7 / Mt 16:19.

[6] See Jn 10:11, 14-16 (RSV-CE).

As with the "keys," the "chair," "binding and loosing," and other Jewish terminology, the Jews immediately recognized Jesus' usage of the terms "shepherd" and "sheep." By calling Himself the "Good Shepherd," Jesus was again declaring that He had come to restore the Davidic kingdom as a shepherd gathers his flock. This is exactly what God revealed through the Old Testament prophets:

- "Behold the Lord God shall come with strength, and his arm shall rule: Behold his reward is with him and his work is before him. He shall feed his flock like a shepherd: he shall gather together the lambs with his arm, and shall take them up in his bosom, and he himself shall carry them that are with young."[7]
- "Behold I will bring them from the north country, and will gather them from the ends of the earth. . . . Hear the word of the Lord, O ye nations, and declare it in the islands that are afar off, and say: He that scattered Israel will gather him: and he will keep him as the shepherd doth his flock."[8]
- "Behold I myself will seek my sheep, and will visit them. . . . I will feed my sheep: and I will cause them to lie down, saith the Lord God. I will seek that which was lost: and that which was driven away, I will bring again. . . . And they shall know that I the Lord their God am with them, and that they are my people the house of Israel: saith the Lord God."[9]

---

[7] Is 40:10-11.

[8] Jer 31:8, 10.

[9] Ezech 34:11, 15-16, 30 (Ezek in RSV-CE). See also 3 Kings 22:17 (1 Kings in RSV-CE); 2 Para 18:16 (2 Chron in RSV-CE); Zach 10:2 (Zech in RSV-CE); Jud 11:15; Ezech 34:2-3, 5.

Matthew, who incorporates the Old Testament concepts in his Gospel more than any other evangelist, also connects Jesus' role as Shepherd with scattered Israel when he records the following statements of Jesus:

- "I was not sent but to the sheep that are lost of the house of Israel."[10]
- "Go ye not into the way of the Gentiles, and into the city of the Samaritans enter ye not. But go ye rather to the lost sheep of the house of Israel."[11]

Thus, through the prophets of old, God reveals that He will restore the "house of Israel" as a "shepherd gathers his sheep." Jesus says that He is this Shepherd. In the New Testament, then, Jesus translates the "house of Israel" into the New Israel, the world-wide kingdom of God, the Holy Catholic Church.[12] In the Church, all the nations of the earth are gathered into the one fold of Christ, the Good Shepherd.

Why does the Father send Jesus to be our Shepherd? *So that the New Covenant family may be one.* Jesus prayed for this unity the night He inaugurated the New Covenant, and then laid down His life for His sheep. We read Jesus' priestly prayer for unity in John's Gospel, chapter 17:

Holy Father, keep them in thy name whom thou hast given me; *that they may be one, as we also are.* While I was with them, I kept them in thy name. Those whom thou gavest me have I kept; and none of them is lost, but the son of perdition, that the scripture may be fulfilled.... And not for them only do I pray, but for them also who

---

[10] Mt 15:24.

[11] Mt 10:5-6. See also Jer 32:37, 40 and Ezech 20:34, 37, which reveal that God will gather His people in a New and Everlasting Covenant.

[12] See Gal 6:16.

through their word shall believe in me; *That they all may be one*, as thou, Father, in me, and I in thee; that they also may be one in us; that the world may believe that thou hast sent me. And the glory which thou hast given me, I have given to them; *that they may be one, as we also are one*: I in them, and thou in me; *that they may be made perfect in one*: and the world may know that thou hast sent me, and hast loved them, as thou hast also loved me.[13]

Jesus repeatedly emphasizes His desire for unity within the Christian family. The unity Jesus prays for concerns both our union with Him and our union with one another as well. Just as we are to love God and neighbor, we are also to be united in truth to God and neighbor. The unity in the Church reflects the truth that binds the faithful together. We are all members of the same body of Christ. If there is a lack of unity, there must necessarily be a *lack of truth* as well, since the truth is not divisive, but one. The thousands of Protestant denominations testify to this reality. Moreover, since truth is universal, the unity must also be universal, or "catholic."

Jesus uses His relationship with the Father to express the unity He desires. Why? First, because Jesus and the Father are perfectly united, which means that nothing short of perfect unity in His Church is acceptable to our Lord. Second, because God is pure truth, and unity subsists in the truth. This is why Paul calls the Church "the pillar and ground of the truth."[14]

Jesus believed that Christian unity was so important that He said it would be the sign to the world that He was truly sent by the Father (see v. 23). If Christ's Church would remain unified in a broken and divided world, people would come to believe in its

[13] Jn 17:11-12, 20-23.
[14] 1 Tim 3:15.

divine institution and save their souls. If the Church were divided, she and her members would fall (see Mk 3:25).

Notice also the subtle parallels in John's Gospel between chapter 10 (where Jesus declares Himself the Good Shepherd) and chapter 17 (where Jesus prays for Christian unity). In John 10, Jesus says that He "giveth his life for his sheep" (v. 11). Jesus analogizes this to a shepherd who guards his sheep from the thief who comes in to steal and kill (see v. 10), and the wolf that snatches them (see v. 12). The good shepherd will sacrifice his life to protect his sheep from evil intruders.

In John 17, Jesus is the Good Shepherd who is about to lay down His life for the sheep *the very next day*. Jesus tells the Father that He has guarded them, like a shepherd, and none is lost but "the son of perdition" (v. 12). Jesus also prays the Father that He should keep them from evil (see v. 15). Just like the earthly shepherd protects his sheep from physical danger, Jesus protects His sheep from spiritual danger by the grace He won for us through His sacrificial death.

Further, in John 10, Jesus says: "And other sheep I have, that are not of this fold: them also I must bring, and they shall hear my voice, and there shall be one fold and one shepherd" (v. 16). Jesus makes a similar statement in John 17: "And not for them only do I pray, but for them also who through their word shall believe in me" (v. 20). Again, Jesus prays for unity within His fold, and desires to bring outsiders into His fold, which is the Church. As John 10 and 17 demonstrate, *Jesus attributes the unity He desires with having one shepherd over His people.*

Because Jesus the Good Shepherd would eventually ascend to the Father and no longer be physically present to shepherd His people, how would Jesus ensure the ongoing unity He prayed for? Would it be by giving His people a Bible three centuries after His ascension (which would not be distributed to the masses until the printing press was invented in the fifteenth century)? No.

Jesus would appoint an earthly shepherd over His people, just as God did in the Old Covenant. Even though the Jews had their Old Testament Scriptures, God appointed shepherds over them to rule and guide them. While they had God's written Word, they needed divinely appointed shepherds to help them interpret the Word. It is no surprise that God does the same thing in the New Covenant.

Even non-Catholics recognize the need for shepherds. They appoint pastors over their communities to maintain uniformity in teaching and discipline. Yet these same people reject the papacy and argue that the Bible is their only authority. If that is the case, then why appoint a pastor? Why not stay at home and read the Bible on one's own?

One wonders why it is so difficult for them to imagine that Christ founded one universal Church and appointed one pastor over it, when they imitate the Catholic model in their own local communities. If they recognize the need for unity in their local "churches," how much more would God institute a plan for unity in His universal, Catholic Church?

As the Bible teaches, Jesus implemented this plan by appointing Peter as the chief shepherd. Like the other divine roles that Jesus delegated to Peter, Jesus would also delegate His role as shepherd to Peter. Peter would unite all of the sheep into one fold while Jesus was in heaven. This brings to completion Ezekiel's prophesy: "And my servant David shall be king over them, and they shall have one shepherd."[15] Just as the Davidic kingdom had a king and a chief shepherd, the Davidic kingdom fulfilled in Christ also has a King (Jesus) and a chief shepherd (Peter).

Only the Catholic Church has the unity Christ prayed for. Why? *Because only the Catholic Church has one shepherd (Peter and his successors).* Unity is measured by one's union with the shepherd. If there is only one shepherd, there can only be one true fold. If

---

[15] Ezech 37:24.

there are multiple shepherds, there will be many folds (as we see in Protestantism). Where there is a lack of unity, there must also be the presence of error, because the truth is indivisible and one. God has answered Jesus' prayer for unity through the papacy of the Catholic Church.

Let us now turn to John's Gospel, chapter 21, and examine Jesus' appointment of Peter as the chief shepherd of the Church.

Jesus Appoints Peter to Shepherd the Church

After His resurrection, Jesus revealed Himself by the sea of Tiberius, where Peter and some of the apostles were fishing. During the evening, the apostles caught nothing. As the day was breaking and the apostles drew near to shore, Jesus stood on the beach and asked the apostles if they had any fish. Not recognizing who Jesus was, the apostles answered "No" (v. 5). Jesus then said: "Cast the net on the right side of the ship, and you shall find" (v. 6). They did so, and they were not able to haul in the number of fish. Yet, the net was not torn.

When Peter discovered that it was Jesus on the shore, he sprang into the sea to greet His Master (see v. 7). Peter then hauled the net of fish ashore, which fed Jesus and the apostles (see vv. 11-12). Peter acts as the shepherd who feeds the flock and leads the flock to Christ. The net that catches fish of every kind but does not break is a metaphor for the Church, the kingdom of heaven, to which Peter has the keys.[16] After they eat together, which ratifies God's covenant bond with His people, Jesus formally designates Peter *alone* as the chief shepherd of the sheep, and charges Peter to feed them and rule over them:

> When they had finished breakfast, Jesus said to Simon Peter, "Simon, son of John, do you love me more than

---

[16] See Mt 13:47-48.

these?" He said to him, "Yes, Lord; you know that I love you." He said to him, "*Feed my lambs.*" A second time he said to him, "Simon, son of John, do you love me?" He said to him, "Yes, Lord; you know that I love you." He said to him, "*Tend my sheep.*" He said to him the third time, "Simon, son of John, do you love me?" Peter was grieved because he said to him the third time, "Do you love me?" And he said to him, "Lord, you know everything; you know that I love you." Jesus said to him, "*Feed my sheep.*"[17]

In the presence of the apostles, Jesus asks Peter: "Do you love me *more than these?*" (v. 15). When Jesus says "more than these," He is referring to the other apostles who were present.[18] Jesus requires Peter to confess His *unique* love for Jesus, and Jesus responds by giving Peter a *unique* role in the Church. His confession and new role is distinguishable from that of "these" other apostles.

We see how the Lord says "tend *my* lambs" and "feed *my* sheep." Jesus does not say "tend *these* sheep" or "feed *those* lambs." Jesus makes it clear that, even though Peter is in charge, it is still Jesus' Church and Jesus' flock. Peter is Jesus' Vicar and His co-pastor. As such, Peter shares in Jesus' universal jurisdiction over the Church, and no one is exempt from his authority. Peter's authority is exercised in the name of the Good Shepherd Himself.

Jesus also requires Peter to make a three-fold affirmation of His love for Jesus. This is to reverse Peter's three-fold denial of Jesus during the Passion. Jesus restores Peter to the grace and gifts that He had promised Peter in Matthew 16:18-19. With his own house in order, Peter can now be the caretaker of the House of God.

Further, Jesus and the apostles taught that two or three witnesses would verify every truth.[19] Jesus requires "three witnesses"

---

[17] Jn 21:15-17 (RSV-CE).

[18] John, James, Nathaniel, Thomas, and two other disciples were present (Jn 21:2).

[19] See Mt 18:16; Jn 5:36-39; 8:13-18; Heb 6:13-18.

from Peter to verify his love for Jesus and commitment to the distinguished office he is now receiving. We may also equate Peter's proclamations with the three witnesses of God's revelation (Scripture, Tradition, Magisterium[20]), the three-fold nature of Peter's office (rock, keys, binding/loosing), and God Himself (Father, Son, Holy Spirit), who will help Peter fulfill his duties.

Jesus requires Peter's profession of love as a requirement for his new responsibilities. God required the same thing from Abraham. Before Abraham became the rock and shepherd of God's covenant people, God had tested Abraham's love for Him by telling him to slay his son Isaac (see Gen 22:2). Abraham demonstrated his unfailing love for God by obeying God's command.

Because of Abraham's love for God, God spared Isaac's life and promised Abraham that the world would be blessed through his seed.[21] God then designated Abraham as the shepherd and father of Israel. Jesus also secures Peter's consent to be the shepherd and father of the New Israel, the Church, through his confession of love for Jesus. Peter and Abraham are required to pledge their love to God before they are entrusted with shepherding His covenant people.

God required a similar thing from David. Before God gave David a successor to his throne, He moved David to repent of his sin of adultery and murder. Once David repented and atoned for his sins, God gave him Solomon to succeed him, and the Davidic kingdom was firmly established.[22]

Finally, Jesus encapsulates His appointment of Peter as chief shepherd by predicting Peter's death. Immediately after ordering Peter to tend the flock, Jesus says:

> "Truly, truly, I say to you, when you were young, you
> girded yourself and walked where you would; but when

---

[20] The word "Magisterium" is Latin for "teaching office."
[21] See Gen 22:16-18.
[22] See 2 Kings 12:20, 24 (2 Sam in RSV-CE).

you are old, you will stretch out your hands, and another
will gird you and carry you where you do not wish to go."
(This he said to show by what death he was to glorify
God.) And after this he said to him, "Follow me."[23]

Jesus emphasizes that the role of chief shepherd is one of service and self-sacrifice, even unto death. The shepherd lays his life
down for the sheep. Just as Abraham was willing to sacrifice Isaac,
so Peter, as chief shepherd, would be willing to lay down his own
life for Christ. Peter would indeed respond to Jesus' invitation:
"Follow me" (Jn 21:19). Peter writes about his pending death in
2 Peter 1:14, looking to the day when he will fulfill his promise to
Jesus: "I will lay down my life for thee."[24] Both Abraham's and
Peter's sacrifice point to the sacrifice of the true Good Shepherd,
Jesus Christ.

Was Peter Ever in Rome?

Speaking of Peter's death, tradition tells us that Peter was martyred in Rome around A.D. 67. Declaring that he was not worthy
to die like Jesus, Peter chose to be crucified upside down. Peter's
bones are kept beneath the altar of St. Peter's Basilica in Rome.
Because Rome was considered the center of the ancient world,
Jesus directed Peter to found the Church in Rome.

To deny the authority of the bishop of Rome (who is the successor of Peter), some non-Catholics argue that Peter was never in
Rome. Whether Peter was ever in Rome is irrelevant to whether
Jesus instituted the papacy. Moreover, this contention flies in the
face of the plethora of historical and extra-biblical evidence
demonstrating that Peter was in Rome. In fact, no one ever gen-
uinely questioned Peter's presence in Rome until the Protestant

---

[23] Jn 21:18-19 (RSV-CE)
[24] Jn 13:37.

Reformation of the sixteenth century (even Martin Luther acknowledged the primacy of the Church at Rome). Nevertheless, the Scriptures also indicate that Peter was in Rome.

In 1 Peter 5:13, Peter says that he is writing his epistle from "Babylon," which was a code name for Rome. The early Christians used code names for things of the faith to avoid Roman persecution. Several verses in the Apocalypse (Revelation), which John wrote while the Church was being persecuted by the Romans, also demonstrate that "Babylon" meant Rome.[25] The sacred writers had scriptural precedent for using this secret name for Rome. In the Old Testament, Babylon, under King Nebuchadnezzar, persecuted the people of God.[26] Other sacred writers began to use the name "Babylon" to refer to any pagan nation that persecuted God's people.[27] Since the Romans persecuted the Church that represented the New Covenant people of God, the city of Rome became known as "Babylon."

When Paul writes his letter to the Romans, he says in chapter 15 (RSV-CE) that he doesn't want to "build on another man's foundation" (v. 20). Paul is referring to Peter, who built the Church in Rome. It would be natural for Paul not to name Peter expressly in his letter, for if it were confiscated by the Romans, Peter's life would be at risk (which his eventual martyrdom proves). Since Paul knew that Peter had already established the Church in Rome, he tells the Romans: "I no longer have any room for work in these regions" (v. 23). Paul also tells the Romans that he will only see them "in passing as I go to Spain" (v. 24) and "I shall go on by way of you to Spain" (v. 28). Paul's nexus with Rome was nominal, because the Roman Church had already been founded by Peter.

---

[25] See Apoc 14:8; 16:19; 17:5; 18:2, 10, 21.

[26] See 4 Kings 24 (2 Kings in RSV-CE).

[27] See Is 13:19; 43:14; Jer 50:29; 51:1-2, 6-9, 11-12, 24, 29-30, 31, 33-35, 37, 41-42, 44, 47-49, 53-56, 58-61, 64.

Peter Must "Feed" the Lambs

In John 21, verses 15 and 17, Jesus says "feed" my lambs. While the Greek word for "feed" (*boskein*) includes a literal nourishing, Jesus primarily has a spiritual feeding in mind. From a Catholic perspective, we understand Jesus' words in the context of the Eucharist, where the priests of the Church feed us with Christ's body and blood. At this time, we recall that Jesus had already instituted the Eucharistic sacrifice with His apostles the night before He died. He took bread, broke it and gave it to His apostles and said: "Take ye, and eat. This is my body. . . . Drink ye all of this. For this is my blood of the new testament, which shall be shed for many unto remission of sins."[28]

Jesus transformed the Old Covenant Passover sacrifice, where the lamb was slain and consumed, to the New Covenant sacrifice of the Eucharist. Jesus is the true Lamb of God, who was slain and now must be consumed. Jesus' teaching that we must eat His flesh and drink His blood is one of His most profound and explicit teachings in Scripture:

> Jesus said to them, "Truly, truly, I say to you, unless you eat the flesh of the Son of man and drink his blood, you have no life in you; he who eats my flesh and drinks my blood has eternal life, and I will raise him up at the last day. For my flesh is food indeed, and my blood is drink indeed. He who eats my flesh and drinks my blood abides in me, and I in him. As the living Father sent me, and I live because of the Father, so he who eats me will live because of me."[29]

---

[28] Mt 26:26, 27-28. Also see Mk 14:22-24; Lk 22:19-20; 1 Cor 11:23-25.

[29] Jn 6:53-57 (RSV-CE). For a thorough study of this topic, please see my book *The Biblical Basis for the Eucharist* (Our Sunday Visitor).

In the Holy Eucharist, Jesus, the Good Shepherd, feeds His lambs and sheep with His own flesh and blood. He nourishes our bodies and our souls. God emphasizes the spiritual aspect of pastoral nourishing through Jeremiah: "And I will give you pastors according to my own heart, and they shall *feed you with knowledge and doctrine*" (Jer 3:15). The next few verses show that God is speaking in the context of His future Church. God reveals that He will take away the Old Covenant practices (see Jer 3:16) and reunite Israel and Juda (see Jer 3:17-18) into a New Covenant family.[30] These pastors of the Church refer to the apostles and their successors, who will feed the people with God's truth (knowledge and doctrine), most especially through the Eucharist.

The Septuagint translation of Jeremiah 3:15 uses a different Greek verb, *poimanao*, for "feed." As we will see in the next section, this word also includes the authority to "rule" over the sheep. It is interesting to note that Jesus tells Peter to "feed" (in Greek, *boske*) the lambs but to both "feed" and "rule" (*poimaine*) the sheep. Is there a difference? A lamb is a baby sheep. A sheep is a grown lamb. Some equate the lambs with the laity and the sheep with the clergy. The laity (lambs) needs to be nourished by the clergy (sheep) so that they can grow to full stature. The sheep are the elder brothers of the flock, and they are responsible for them.

Only the clergy has the power to confect the Eucharist. Only the clergy is directly accountable to the pope for how they carry out their priestly duties. Thus, it makes perfect sense for Jesus to delineate His Vicar's responsibility to feed and rule over the clergy, while only feeding the laity. These are the most immediate and practical aspects of Peter's universal jurisdiction over the Church. Thus, speaking for Christ, Peter tells his fellow clergymen: "So I exhort the elders among you, as a fellow elder and a witness of the

---

[30] Jeremiah is more explicit about the New Covenant in Jer 23:5-6; 31:34; 32:40; 33:15-16.

sufferings of Christ as well as a partaker in the glory that is to be revealed. Tend the flock of God that is your charge, not by constraint but willingly, not for shameful gain but eagerly."[31]

Some non-Catholics look at this passage and say Peter had no authority over the other clergy because he describes himself as "a fellow elder" (v. 1). This is a silly argument. Peter, under divine inspiration, is giving *an order* to the clergy to tend the flock of God. Peter issues the order by saying "I *exhort* the elders" (v. 1). This would certainly be presumptuous if Peter had no authority over them.

We might also ask why Peter's humility undermines his authority. Jesus describes Himself as "meek, and humble of heart" (Mt 11:29). By calling himself a fellow elder, Peter is imitating the humility of His Lord, which he also commands his readers to practice.[32] Peter imitated the Lord's humility all the way to his own crucifixion. These non-Catholics would not argue that the president of the United States undermines his authority when he says "My fellow Americans." Nor should they argue the same regarding Peter.

Peter Must "Rule" Over the Sheep

As we have mentioned, in John 21:16 Jesus tells Peter to "rule" (in Greek, *poimainein*) the sheep.[33] This is a significant verse because, like many other verses, it demonstrates that Peter *has authority over the other apostles.* Like feeding, ruling is a part of being a shepherd. The shepherd must nourish his flock, but he must also discipline his flock as well. The shepherd has complete authority over the sheep.

---

[31] 1 Pet 5:1-2 (RSV-CE).
[32] See 1 Pet 3:8; 5:5-6.
[33] RSV-CE.

The Septuagint translation of the Old Testament uses the verbal form of "to shepherd" (in Greek, *poimanao*, from the Hebrew, *raah*) in various places. In the following examples, "shepherd" is used to describe both "feeding" and "ruling":

- "Thou shalt *feed* my people Israel, and thou shalt be *prince* over Israel."[34]
- "I took thee out of the *pastures* from following the sheep to be *ruler* over my people Israel."[35]
- "Thou shalt *feed* my people Israel, and thou shalt be *ruler* over them."[36]
- "And he *fed* them in the innocence of his heart: and *conducted* them by the skilfulness of his hands."[37]
- "*Feed* thy people with thy rod, the flock of thy inheritance, them that dwell alone in the forest, in the midst of Carmel: they shall *feed* in Basan and Galaad according to the days of old."[38]

We see a similar use in the Acts of the Apostles when Paul exhorts the bishops: "Take heed to yourselves, and to the whole flock, wherein the [Holy Spirit] hath placed you bishops, to *rule* the church of God, which he hath purchased with his own blood" (Acts 20:28). Peter also combines feeding with ruling when he says: "*Feed* the flock of God which is among you, taking care of it, not by *constraint*, but willingly, according to God: not for filthy lucre's sake, but voluntarily: Neither as *lording* it over the clergy, but being made a pattern of the flock from the heart."[39]

---

[34] 2 Kings 5:2.
[35] 2 Kings 7:8.
[36] 1 Para 11:2 (1 Chron in RSV-CE).
[37] Ps 77(78):72
[38] Mich 7:14 (Mic in RSV-CE).
[39] 1 Pet 5:2-3.

Psalm 2:9's use of *poimanao* emphasizes the powerful, authoritative, and definitive nature of a shepherd's ruling: "Thou shalt *rule* them with a rod of iron, and shalt *break* them in pieces like a potter's vessel." In this case, ruling refers to a type of destruction. This is the same word that the Apocalypse uses several times to describe Jesus' ruling over the churches. In fact, the following verses quote from Psalm 2:9:

- "And he shall *rule* them with a rod of iron, and as the vessel of a potter they shall be broken" (Apoc 2:27).
- "And she brought forth a man child, who was to *rule* all nations with an iron rod: and her son was taken up to God, and to his throne" (Apoc 12:5).
- "And he shall *rule* them with a rod of iron; and he treadeth the winepress of the fierceness of the wrath of God the Almighty" (Apoc 19:15).

This last verse from the Apocalypse is particularly powerful because it associates *poimanao* with the authority to *bring down God's wrath*. This is the ultimate meaning of "ruling with a rod of iron." By telling Peter to "rule" the flock, Jesus is giving Peter the authority to make divine judgments over the entire Church in the name of God. Those who oppose Peter's authority will be "dashed into pieces" with severe punishments. This is another biblical example of Peter's authority to make binding and loosing decisions, which God will confirm in heaven.

Peter Must Strengthen the Other Apostles

As we have seen, Jesus gives Peter alone the title of rock, the keys to the kingdom of heaven, and the charge to rule over the other apostles. In Luke's Gospel, Jesus gives Peter another unique role to fulfill. Right after Jesus institutes the Eucharist and the New Covenant priesthood, Jesus tells Peter *to strengthen the other apostles*:

"Simon, Simon, behold, Satan demanded to have you, that he might sift you like wheat, but I have prayed for you that your faith may not fail; and when you have turned again, strengthen your brethren."[40]

This is another powerful example of Peter's primacy among the apostles. Up to this point, Jesus has been addressing all of the apostles collectively. For example, in Luke 22:27-30, right before Jesus tells Peter to confirm the apostles, Jesus tells His apostles:

For which is greater, he that sitteth at table, or he that serveth? Is not he that sitteth at table? But I am in the midst of *you* [in Greek, *humon*, plural] as he that serveth: And *you* [*humeis*, plural] are they who have continued with me in my temptations: And I dispose to *you* [*humin*, plural], as my Father hath disposed to me, a kingdom; That you may eat and drink at my table, in my kingdom: and may sit upon thrones, judging the twelve tribes of Israel.

After Jesus explains to the apostles their roles as servants in the Church (the kingdom), He turns His attention exclusively to Peter. In Luke 22:31, Jesus tells Peter (and no one else) how Satan desires to attack the apostles: "Satan demanded to *have you* [Greek, *humas*, plural], that he might *sift you* [*siniasai*, plural] like wheat." Then Jesus tells Peter alone: "But I have prayed for *you* [*sou*, singular] that *your* [*sou*, singular] faith may not fail; and when *you* [*su*, singular] have turned again, strengthen *your* [*sou*, singular] brethren" (v. 32).

Why does Jesus single out Peter to tell him about Satan's desire for the apostles? *Because Peter is in charge of them.* This is demonstrated by the fact that Jesus prays for Peter *alone*, and

---

[40] Lk 22:31-32 (RSV-CE)

charges Peter *alone* to confirm, or strengthen the other apostles. Jesus does not tell anyone else to strengthen the apostles. Nor does Jesus tell anyone to strengthen Peter, which He Himself will do directly through the charism He gives to Peter's office.

This is further proof of Peter's infallibility. Jesus specifically prays that Peter's faith will not fail. Jesus is referring to Peter's faith in the context of his teaching authority, which is the most important aspect of Peter's role as chief shepherd of the Church. The fact that Jesus is speaking of Peter's faith in the context of his leadership of the Church is demonstrated by His immediately preceding explanations of the apostles' roles within the Church (as Eucharistic servants and judges). This is also demonstrated by Jesus' directive to Peter to confirm the other apostles, who represent the foundation of the Church.

Jesus is also referring to Peter's faith vis-à-vis the power of Satan and his hell. Since Satan desires to tear down the Church (by sifting its leaders like wheat), Jesus assures us that the gates of hell will not prevail against the Church (see Mt 16:18). Peter's faith as the rock of the Church and chief shepherd of the flock will triumph over the devil and his minions. Jesus' prayer for Peter assures us of this result, since Jesus' prayers are always answered by the Father. If not, Jesus' prayer would have been in vain, and He would have built a Church that He knew was destined for failure. This, of course, is something God would never do, for God cannot deceive us.

Thus, Jesus is not referring to Peter's "personal" faith. God does not assure Peter or any of us that our personal faith in Christ will not fail. God respects our free will to reject Him. God even allowed Peter to deny Christ three times before he ultimately became "converted," as Jesus alludes to in Luke 22:32. Ascending to the throne of Peter does not guarantee a pope's admission into heaven. It guarantees that the pope will not officially teach the

Church anything that will deter our journey to heaven. This is because it is guaranteed by the prayer of Jesus Christ Himself.

The supernatural quality of Peter's faithful leadership is demonstrated by Jesus' use of the word "strengthen" (see Lk 22:32). Jesus prays that Peter will "strengthen" (in Greek, *sterixo*) the other apostles. This word means to fix or establish, and it is always used in connection with imparting spiritual graces. For example, Paul tells the Romans: "For I long to see you, that I may impart unto you some spiritual grace, to *strengthen* [in Greek, *sterixthesai*] you" (Rom 1:11). Paul also writes: "And we sent Timothy, our brother, and the minister of God in the gospel of Christ, to *confirm* [*sterixai*] you and exhort you concerning your faith" (1 Thess 3:2).

Paul also uses the word to describe how God and Jesus strengthen us in His grace:

- "Now to him that is able to *establish* you, according to my gospel, and the preaching of Jesus Christ, according to the revelation of the mystery, which was kept secret from eternity" (Rom 16:25).
- "Now our Lord Jesus Christ himself, and God and our Father, who hath loved us, and hath given us everlasting consolation, and good hope in grace, exhort your hearts, and *confirm* you in every good work and word."[41]
- "But God is faithful, who will *strengthen* and keep you from evil."[42]

By commanding Peter to "confirm" his brethren, Jesus is giving Peter the ability to impart divine graces through the office he exercises. Peter is the immovable rock, the keeper of the keys, and a conduit of grace for the rest of the apostles. Peter, the Vicar of

---

[41] 2 Thess 2:15-16.
[42] 2 Thess 3:3.

Christ, will impart the graces of Christ to the apostles, which they will need to fulfill their vocations as shepherds of the flock. Peter will do this through his teaching authority and pastoral leadership. We recall that God fixed the chief steward of the Davidic kingdom "as a peg in a sure place."[43] Now, through the grace of the office of Peter (the chief steward of the New Covenant kingdom), God will do the same for the apostles.

---

[43] Is 22:23.

CHAPTER SIX

⟨∾∾⟩

Peter Is the Leader of the Early Church

While Jesus was on earth, He was the visible source of unity among the apostles. But after Jesus "was lifted up, and a cloud took him out of their sight,"[1] Peter became the spokesman for Christ, just as Jesus had appointed him. Immediately after the Ascension, we find the apostles gathered in prayer with the Blessed Virgin Mary and the other disciples in the Upper Room (about one hundred twenty people).[2] This was the sacred place where Jesus instituted the Eucharist and appeared to His apostles after His resurrection.[3] This was the first assembly of the infant Church.

We must remember that there was not a letter of New Testament Scripture written at this point. In fact, the first book of the New Testament would not be written for at least another decade, and the Bible as we know it would not be officially compiled for another three hundred fifty years. Yet the Church was alive and well, because she was guided by Peter, her chief shepherd. Peter would now be the visible source of unity for the Christian family, and he would hand on the teachings of Christ under the guidance of the Holy Spirit. We now look at the examples of Peter's leadership in the Church as the evangelist Luke recorded them in the Acts of the Apostles.

---

[1] Acts 1:9 (RSV-CE).
[2] See Acts 1:15.
[3] See Acts 1:12-14.

Peter Chooses a Successor to Judas

The Acts of the Apostles begins with Peter's first binding decision as the teacher of the Church. It concerns choosing a successor to Judas Iscariot, who committed suicide after betraying Jesus. As the infant Church was assembled in the Upper Room, Peter "stood up among the brethren" to issue his teaching that a successor would be required.[4] Peter bases his decision upon his interpretation of Psalm 68:26 (69:25) and Psalm 108(109):8, which he quotes to the assembly from memory: "For it is written in the book of Psalms: Let their habitation become desolate, and let there be none to dwell therein. And his bishopric let another take" (Acts 1:20).

After Peter makes his decision, the apostles put forward two men, Barsabbas and Matthias, from whom to choose.[5] After they pray to the Lord for guidance, they cast lots to make their decision. The lot falls on Matthias, who is then enrolled with the eleven.[6]

Peter's action reveals his divine authority over the Church. We see that Peter "stood up" among the assembly of one hundred twenty people (Acts 1:15). This is an explicit display of authority, and not one among the large crowd of believers questions it. The people are accustomed to being taught by Jesus, and now they look to Peter. Peter has replaced Moses as the seat of authority in Israel, and the people know it. Peter's decision sets the precedent for how the Church will be governed going forward — namely, through his authoritative leadership. Further, Peter's decision also sets the apostolic wheels in motion, as he inaugurates a system of succession in the Church for future generations.

The manner in which Peter renders his decision is telling. Peter uses the Psalms as the basis for his decision. However, the

---

[4] Acts 1:15.
[5] See Acts 1:23.
[6] See Acts 1:26.

Psalms upon which he relies (Ps 68:26; 108:8) say absolutely nothing about the betrayer of Christ or apostolic succession at all. Since other Scriptures speak of Judas' betrayal and succession to office, Peter could have relied upon them. Instead, Peter uses two obscure Psalms and sets forth his definitive interpretation of them.

This means that Peter has received divine guidance from God regarding their meaning. We recall that Peter has had no formal training as a rabbi. Scripture describes him as "illiterate and ignorant" (Acts 4:13). Yet we also recall that God was able to intrude into Peter's mind about the nature of Jesus as the Christ and Son of God, and Peter was able to articulate that truth without error (see Mt 16:18).

In the same way, God penetrates the mind of Peter, which allows him to render an infallible interpretation of the Psalms, and no one questions his interpretation. God will continue to guide Peter to make other error-free pronouncements for the good of the Church. Peter and his successors will possess a divine understanding of Scripture, and the authority to make definitive judgments as to their meaning.

Peter Preaches on Pentecost

As Jesus has promised, He sends the Holy Spirit to the apostles on Pentecost Sunday, which is considered the birthday of the Church. The Holy Spirit descends upon the apostles in the form of tongues of fire, and they begin to speak in other tongues.[7] When the twelve apostles go out into Jerusalem and begin speaking in the languages of fifteen nations, outsiders begin to accuse them of drunkenness. The crowd says: "These men are full of new wine" (Acts 2:13).

Once again, Peter assumes his leadership of the Church and speaks to the crowd on behalf of the apostles. Peter explains the

---

[7] See Acts 2:1-4.

significance of the gathering of the nations and the miracle of the tongue-speaking by rendering another infallible interpretation of Scripture. This time Peter quotes from the prophet Joel:

> And it shall come to pass, in the last days, (saith the Lord,) I will pour out of my Spirit upon all flesh: and your sons and your daughters shall prophesy, and your young men shall see visions, and your old men shall dream dreams. And upon my servants indeed, and upon my handmaids will I pour out in those days of my spirit, and they shall prophesy.[8]

The verses from the prophet Joel do not specifically define the "last days" as the ten days after the ascension of the Messiah, yet Peter applies them to Pentecost Sunday. The verses are also not explicit about tongue-speaking, yet Peter applies them to the miracle they have experienced. Again, no one questions Peter's interpretation.

Peter continues his teaching by infallibly interpreting another Scripture, this time Psalm 15(16):9-10: "For this my heart hath been glad, and any tongue hath rejoiced: moreover my flesh also shall rest in hope. Because thou wilt not leave my soul in hell, nor suffer thy Holy One to see corruption."[9] Although the Psalm does not expressly refer to the Messiah, Peter declares that David was writing about Jesus Christ (see Acts 2:31-32).

Peter supports his conclusion by quoting from Psalm 109 110):1: "The Lord said to my Lord, sit thou at my right hand, until I make thy enemies thy footstool."[10] This is the same passage Jesus used to confound the Pharisees when they tested Him.[11]

---

[8] Acts 2:17-18; see Joel 2:28-29.
[9] Acts 2:26-27.
[10] Acts 2:34-35.
[11] See Mt 22:41-46; Mk 12:35-37; Lk 20:41-44

Peter now renders a definitive interpretation of this confusing passage, declaring that the "Lord of my Lord" is Jesus Christ: "Therefore let all the house of Israel know most certainly, that God hath made both Lord and Christ, this same Jesus, whom you have crucified" (Acts 2:36).

These are bold and riveting declarations made by Peter. But far from questioning Peter or his authority to interpret Scripture, Luke says that the people "had compunction in their heart" (Acts 2:37). Peter, guided by the Spirit, declares the true meaning of these centuries-old Scriptures, and the crowd is moved to conversion. They ask Peter and the apostles: "What shall we do, men and brethren?" (Acts 2:37). Peter again speaks on behalf of the apostles and declares: "Repent, and be baptized every one of you in the name of Jesus Christ for the forgiveness of your sins; and you shall receive the gift of the Holy Spirit. For the promise is to you and to your children and to all that are far off, every one whom the Lord our God calls to him."[12]

Thus, Peter is the first person in the early Church to preach repentance and the need for water baptism for the forgiveness of sins. As the Vicar of Christ, Peter speaks on behalf of Jesus, who said: "He that believeth and is baptized, shall be saved: but he that believeth not shall be condemned."[13] As a result of Peter's definitive teachings and exhortations, about three thousand people are baptized on that first Pentecost Sunday (see Acts 2:41). As Luke says, the people *"received his word,"* in reference to Peter (Acts 2:41). Peter, the chief shepherd, leads the early Church by speaking for Christ and bringing His sheep into the one fold.

---

[12] Acts 2:38-39 (RSV-CE). In verse 39, the Greek word for children is *teknon*. This is the same word used to describe eight-day old infants in Acts 21:21. This demonstrates that water baptism is for infants as well as adults.

[13] Mk 16:16; see also Mt 28:19.

Peter Works the First Healing

The next instance of Peter's divine authority is the healing of a man who was lame from his mother's womb. The lame man has begged for alms every day at the gate of the temple. After Peter's first sermon and the baptism of the three thousand, Peter and John go to the temple to pray. As they approach the temple, the lame man asks them for alms.

Although he asks both Peter and John, Peter alone declares to the beggar: "Silver and gold I have none; but what I have, I give thee: In the name of Jesus Christ of Nazareth, arise, and walk" (Acts 3:6). Then Peter takes him by the hand, lifts him up, and the man is able to walk. The man goes into the temple, leaping and praising God, and the people are filled with wonder and amazement. Peter has performed the first physical healing in the Church age.[14]

As the people stand in wonder, Peter declares that it was not through his own power, but the power of Jesus Christ and His resurrection that the lame man was cured (see Acts 3:12-16). Peter then exhorts the crowd to repentance by saying, "Be penitent, therefore, and be converted, that your sins may be blotted out" (Acts 3:19). This is reminiscent of Jesus' cure of the man with palsy. After Jesus cured him physically, He cured him spiritually by saying: "Son, thy sins are forgiven thee."[15] As the Vicar of Christ, Peter follows Jesus' formula by seeking a spiritual healing to follow the physical healing.

In explaining to the crowd the truth of Jesus, Peter once again interprets the Scriptures. Peter first quotes from Moses' book of

---

[14] Through the power of the keys, Peter continued to effect supernatural healings in the Church, for example: healing the sick with his shadow (Acts 5:15); curing Aeneas of his palsy (Acts 9:33-34); and raising Tabitha from the dead (Acts 9:36-41).

[15] Mk 2:5; see Lk 5:20; Mt 9:2.

Deuteronomy: "A prophet shall the Lord your God raise up unto you of your brethren, like unto me: him you shall hear according to all things whatsoever he shall speak to you. And it shall be, that every soul which will not hear that prophet, shall be destroyed from among the people" (Acts 3:22-23).[16] And after referring to the prophets and Samuel and those who followed him, Peter quotes from the book of Genesis: "And in thy seed shall all the kindreds of the earth be blessed" (Act 3:25).

As in his sermon on Pentecost, Peter sets forth a definitive interpretation of the Jewish Scriptures. He declares that Jesus is the prophet revealed through Moses, through whom all the people of the earth will be blessed. While these Scripture verses are not explicitly Messianic, Peter judges them as pointing to Jesus. Peter is the authentic interpreter of God's Word in the New Covenant, just as Moses was in the Old, from whom Peter quotes. Peter demonstrates that he holds the keys to the kingdom of heaven. Peter "looses" the lame man from his physical bondage, and then "binds" the people to His teachings.

As Peter preaches about Jesus and the resurrection, Peter and John are apprehended by the Jewish leaders and brought before the high priest. They ask both Peter and John: "By what power, or by what name, have you done this?" (Acts 4:7). Peter once again speaks for the Church, declaring that it is by the power of Jesus raised from the dead that the lame man was cured (see Acts 4:10). Peter then sets forth another infallible interpretation of the Psalms, when he says: "This is the stone which was rejected by you the builders, which is become the head of the corner. Neither is there salvation in any other. For there is no other name under heaven given to men, whereby we must be saved" (Acts 4:11-12).[17]

---

[16] See Dt 18:18-19.
[17] See Ps 117(118):22.

Through his authoritative teaching and courage, *Peter unites the infant Church*. Luke tells that the whole Church was filled with the Holy Spirit, and had but *one heart and soul* (see Acts 4:31-32). This is because they had *one* shepherd, Peter. They also sold their possessions and brought the money to the apostles, holding everything in common (see Acts 4:32-35). While God gave the other apostles the ability to work miracles, they could only do so by virtue of their union with Peter. Peter was the unifying force in this early Christian community, through the grace that Jesus gave him as shepherd of the flock.

Peter Condemns Ananias and Sapphira

Peter's condemnation of Ananias and Sapphira is one of the most explicit examples of his binding authority. In chapter 5 of the Acts of the Apostles, we learn that Ananias and his wife Sapphira have sold a piece of land, and have laid the proceeds "at the feet of the apostles" (v. 2). But unlike the other members of the early Church, they have fraudulently withheld a portion of the purchase price for themselves.

Speaking on behalf of the Church, Peter declares to Ananias: "Why has Satan filled your heart to lie to the Holy Spirit and to keep back part of the proceeds of the land? While it remained unsold, did it not remain your own? And after it was sold, was it not at your disposal? How is it that you have contrived this deed in your heart? You have not lied to men but to God."[18]

Peter's declaration is extremely significant. It shows that God has revealed to Peter Ananias' sinful conduct, just as God has revealed to Peter the meaning of Scripture. God gives Peter theological and moral insights (which represent Peter's infallibility on matters of faith and morals). God is *working with* Peter while he

---

[18] Acts 5:3-4 (RSV-CE).

is the steward of Christ's Church.[19] With this divine guidance, Peter renders a binding judgment against Ananias for the good of the Church, which brings about his death: "When Ananias heard these words, he fell down and died. And great fear came upon all who heard of it."[20]

Three hours later, Sapphira comes to the apostles, not knowing what has happened to her husband. After questioning Sapphira and catching her in the same lie, Peter pronounces a binding judgment against her as well: "Why have you agreed together to tempt the Spirit of the Lord? Behold the feet of them who have buried thy husband are at the door, and they shall carry thee out. Immediately she fell down before his feet, and gave up the ghost. And the young men coming in, found her dead: and carried her out, and buried her by her husband" (vv. 9-10).

As this story demonstrates, Peter has the definitive and final authority to determine when a member of the Church has sinned, *and* what punishment should be imposed. By having the "keys of death and hell," Peter exercises plenary and supernatural authority in the realm of faith (doctrine) and morals (discipline). What Peter binds on earth is bound in heaven. When Peter binds Ananias and Sapphira in their sins against the Holy Spirit, heaven reciprocates by bringing about their death. Peter pronounces his judgments as the leader of the Church, for Luke says: "And there came great fear upon *the whole church*, and upon all that heard these things" (Acts 5:11).

Later in the book of Acts, Peter also judges the sinful conduct of a man named Simon, who is a recent convert of the Church. In chapter 8, Luke describes how Peter and John come to the town of Samaria to give the sacrament of confirmation to the faithful.[21]

---

[19] For Scriptures that teach that God "works with" (from the Greek, *sunergei*) his apostles, see Mk 16:20; Rom 8:28; 1 Cor 3:9; 2 Cor 6:1.

[20] Acts 5:5 (RSV-CE).

Luke says: "For it [the Holy Spirit] had not yet fallen on any of them, but they had only been baptized in the name of the Lord Jesus. Then they laid their hands on them and they received the Holy Spirit."[22]

When Simon sees that people receive the Holy Spirit by the imposition of the apostles' hands, he offers the apostles money, saying: "Give me also this power, that any one on whom I lay my hands may receive the Holy Spirit."[23] Peter declares to Simon: "Your silver perish with you, because you thought you could obtain the gift of God with money! You have neither part nor lot in this matter, for your heart is not right before God. Repent therefore of this wickedness of yours, and pray to the Lord that, if possible, the intent of your heart may be forgiven you. For I see that you are in the gall of bitterness and in the bond of iniquity."[24]

This case is different from that of Ananias and Sapphira because Peter does not condemn Simon to death. But Scripture might give us an insight why. We have already discussed how the apostles' authority to bind and loose includes the authority to judge the sincerity of the penitent. Peter does this with Simon. Through the divine guidance that God gives him, Peter judges Simon harshly, but recognizes that he has the ability to repent. Instead of mortally binding Simon in his sins, he tells Simon to do penance and pray for forgiveness. Peter's judgment is correct, for

---

[21] Confirmation is one of the seven sacraments of the Catholic Church. This sacrament brings about the perfection of baptismal graces in a person's soul and enables the person to effectively bear witness to the Gospel in his or her daily life. The early Church conferred this sacrament by laying hands on the baptized Christian as part of the complex of initiation rites beginning with baptism and concluding with the Paschal Eucharist.

[22] Acts 8:16-17 (RSV-CE)

[23] Acts 8:19 (RSV-CE).

[24] Acts 8:20-23 (RSV-CE).

Simon expresses fear of God and repents of his sins. He begs Peter: "Pray you for me to the Lord, that none of these things which you have spoken may come upon me" (Acts 8:24).

Peter Raises Tabitha From the Dead

Another remarkable example of Peter's loosing authority occurred in the city of Joppa. Chapter 9 of Acts says that Peter was visiting all the members of the Church throughout Judea, Galilee, and Samaria (see vv. 31-32). This was the natural thing for the leader of the Church to do. During his travels, Peter cured a man named Aeneas of an eight-year-old affliction of palsy in the city of Lydda (see v. 34).

While Peter was still in Lydda, two members of the Church traveled from the nearby city of Joppa to notify Peter that a special disciple named Tabitha had died (see v. 37). They wished that Peter would come to her bedside in Joppa, and Peter obliged. When he arrived at Tabitha's bedside, the widows were crying over her death. Luke describes what happened next: "And they all being put forth, Peter kneeling down prayed, and turning to the body, he said: Tabitha, arise. And she opened her eyes; and seeing Peter, she sat up. And giving her his hand, he lifted her up. And when he had called the saints and the widows, he presented her alive" (vv. 40-41).

This short story is another incredible example of how Christ acts through His Vicar. Even though Peter was in another city, the disciples sought him and no one else. Why? Because the Church understood that Peter had the keys of "death and hell." Because Peter had the keys, he was able to invoke the authority of Jesus Christ Himself. Jesus acted through Peter in giving life to the Church. Peter decided to "loose" Tabitha from the gates of death, and Jesus ratified Peter's decision in heaven by raising her to new life.

Peter Receives a Revelation and Baptizes Gentiles

In Acts 10, we read another story about Peter and a man named Cornelius, who was a Roman centurion. Cornelius was a very religious man who prayed constantly to God and gave alms to the people. One day, an angel of the Lord visited Cornelius and told him that his prayers and alms ascended as a memorial before God (see v. 4). Because of Cornelius' piety and love for God, the angel told him to send for Peter, who was still in Joppa (see v. 5). Why? Because Peter had the keys to the kingdom of heaven, and it would be through Peter's words that Cornelius and the rest of the Gentiles would be saved.[25] Thus, Cornelius sent two of his household servants to find Peter.

While the servants were en route to Joppa, Peter was in deep prayer and God gave him a vision. In that vision, Peter saw heaven opened and what appeared to be a large linen sheet descend before him. The sheet displayed all kinds of animals, birds, and creeping things of the earth. Then a voice came to Peter: "Arise, Peter; kill and eat" (v. 13). Peter, who had always obeyed the Mosaic law, said: "Far be it from me; for I never did eat any thing that is common and unclean" (v. 14). God responded, "That which God hath cleansed, do not thou call common" (v. 15). Thus, in this vision, God was asking Peter to kill and eat prey that would have been considered unclean under the law of Moses.

As Peter was contemplating this vision, the Holy Spirit told Peter that certain men had just arrived to see him. He commanded Peter to arise and go with these men. Peter obeyed the Lord and met the visitors, who explained to Peter what had happened to Cornelius. They said that God's angel had visited Cornelius and told him to seek out Peter. Peter gave the men lodging for the evening, and he then traveled to Caesarea to see Cornelius the next

---

[25] See Acts 10:44-45.

day. When they arrived, Cornelius paid homage to Peter by falling at his feet (see v. 25).

After Peter commanded him to get up, Peter interpreted the divine vision that God gave him by declaring: "In very deed I perceive, that God is not a respecter of persons. But in every nation, he that feareth him, and worketh justice, is acceptable to him" (vv. 34-35). Then, after proclaiming the truth of Jesus and His resurrection, Peter declared: "To him all the prophets give testimony, that by his name *all receive remission of sins*, who believe in him" (v. 43). After Peter spoke these words, the Holy Spirit descended upon all who heard his word, and the Jews were amazed that God would give such grace to the Gentiles as well (see vv. 44-45).

Then, as he did at Pentecost, Peter commanded the Church to baptize, *but this time the Gentiles*. He said: "'Can any one forbid water for baptizing these people who have received the Holy Spirit just as we have?' And he commanded them to be baptized in the name of Jesus Christ."[26] Through the power of the keys, Peter "loosed" the gates of heaven to the Gentiles.

This was an astonishing event for the Jews of the early Church. God had excluded the Gentiles from His covenant with Moses. Now, based on the divine insights that God gave Peter, Peter was telling the Church that they were included in the New Covenant of Christ. While his vision was full of symbolism, Peter infallibly interpreted it. Then, at Peter's word, the Gentiles received the Holy Spirit and were baptized into Christ's body. As always, no one questioned Peter's authority, even when his decisions seemed novel or unprecedented.

Why is this story so significant? Because it shows that God (1) uses Peter alone (2) by giving him divine insights, (3) which Peter infallibly interprets (4) and communicates to the Church, (5) which forms the basis of his teaching (6) and which the Church

---

[26] Acts10:47-48 (RSV-CE).

obeys without question. We are also reminded of the similarities between Abraham and Peter:

- Abraham was the rock and father of Old Testament Israel / Peter is the rock and father of the New Israel, the Church.
- Abraham gave Israel the covenant of circumcision / Peter gives the Church the New Covenant "circumcision"[27] of baptism.
- Abraham's seed will be forever blessed in the future / Peter brings about this blessing by baptizing both Jews and Gentiles into Christ.

When Peter returned to Jerusalem, the Jews questioned Peter regarding why he was associating with Gentiles, and how they had received the Word of God. Since Peter was leading the Church and making the important decisions, they quite correctly approached Peter. Peter responded by recounting his vision and telling about the visitors from Caesarea. Then Peter orally recalled the words of Jesus: "John baptized with water, but you shall be baptized with the Holy Spirit."[28]

After explaining his divine vision and the words of Christ, Peter humbly set forth his interpretation: "If then God gave them the same grace, as to us also who believed in the Lord Jesus Christ; who was I, that could withstand God?" (Acts 11:17). After Peter spoke, the crowd obediently accepted Peter's teaching. Luke says: "Having heard these things, *they held their peace*, and glorified God, saying: God then hath also to the Gentiles given repentance unto life" (Acts 11:18).

It was only after Peter's definitive teaching about the Gentiles' salvation that Paul began to preach to them about salvation as well. In fact, Paul used the same Psalm that Peter used to explain the res-

---

[27] See Col 2:11-12.
[28] Acts 11:16 (RSV-CE).

urrection of Christ: "Thou shalt not suffer thy holy one to see corruption. But he whom God hath raised from the dead, saw no corruption."[29] Paul and the other apostles followed Peter's teaching and bound the Church to it at the local level (here, Antioch).

Peter Is Freed From Prison by an Angel

Chapter 12 of the Acts of the Apostles presents another example of God's divine intervention in Peter's life. As the Church grew under the leadership of Peter, King Herod persecuted her members. He killed James, the brother of John, and eventually imprisoned Peter. During this time, Luke says that "prayer was made without ceasing by the church unto God for him" (v. 5). The entire Church prayed for Peter because Peter was her leader.

While he was sleeping between two soldiers in the prison, God sent an angel to Peter to free him. The angel struck Peter on the side, raised him up and said: "Arise quickly" (v. 7). Luke reports that "the chains fell off from his hands. And the angel said to him: Gird thyself, and put on thy sandals. And he did so. And he said to him: Cast thy garment about thee, and follow me" (vv. 7-8). The angel led Peter out into the city and departed from him. Peter, once again, was the object of God's divine intervention.

Recognizing that he had just been delivered by God's angel, Peter went to the house of Mary, the mother of John. There the disciples were gathered in prayer. Peter knocked on the door. Rhoda, the housekeeper, recognized Peter's voice and informed the others (see v. 14). (Since Peter constantly spoke for the Church, it is understandable how a disciple could recognize Peter's voice without seeing him.) The disciples, knowing that Peter had been imprisoned, were astonished to see him. Peter told the disciples what had happened, and left. What was the point of Peter's visit? To let the disciples know that the Church was still in his care.

---

[29] Acts 13:35, 37; see Acts 2:26-27.

Of course, Peter is not the only one for whom God had performed such miracles. But this story demonstrates that God continued to work with Peter as he led the fledgling Church. Peter still had significant work to do for the Church, such as rendering his decision at the Council of Jerusalem (discussed next) and establishing his seat of authority in Rome. While other disciples had been martyred, it was too soon for Peter to die. God preserved Peter's leadership in the Church through divine interventions until his mission was completed.

Peter's Decision at the Council of Jerusalem

In Acts 15, we read about the famous Council of Jerusalem. This council made the monumental decision that Gentile Christians did not have to follow the Mosaic law of circumcision to enter into the Church. As we will see, this first council of the Church not only demonstrates that Peter was in charge, but also that the Church did not believe in *sola Scriptura*. Let's examine what happened in some detail.

We recall that the infant Church was exclusively Jewish until Peter unlocked the kingdom to the Gentiles. This happened about ten years after Christ's ascension into heaven. When Gentiles began to enter the Church, many of the Jews believed that the Gentiles had to be circumcised like themselves. This was because God gave Abraham circumcision as a sign of His everlasting covenant with him: "This is my covenant which you shall observe, between me and you, and thy seed after thee: All the male kind of you shall be circumcised."[30] God also renewed this covenant with Moses.[31]

Paul and Barnabas debated this issue with some of the disciples in Judea. After a while, the disciples decided to send Paul and

---

[30] Gen 17:10; see also Gen 17:12, 14, 23-24, 26-27; 21:4; 34:15, 17, 24.
[31] See Lev 12:3.

Barnabas to Jerusalem to meet with Peter and the apostles to resolve the matter. They knew that Peter had the seat of authority in the Church, and their teaching had to be in conformity with his teaching. After "they were received by the Church," they all assembled to consider the question (v. 4). After much disputing, Peter, in another display of authority, "rose up" to settle the matter (see v. 7).

Peter began his discussion by reminding the Church that God specifically chose him, as their leader, to preach the Gospel to the Gentiles that they may believe (see v. 7). Peter then declared that both Jews and Gentiles are saved the same way, through Jesus Christ, not through the yolk of circumcision: "And put no difference between us and them, purifying their hearts by faith. Now therefore, why tempt you God to put a yoke upon the necks of the disciples, which neither our fathers nor we have been able to bear? But by the grace of the Lord Jesus Christ, we believe to be saved, in like manner as they also" (vv. 9-11). After Peter definitively settled the issue, Luke says that "all the multitude held their peace" (v. 12).

After Peter had spoken, Paul and Barnabas, who had debated the issue in Judea, now spoke in support of Peter's teaching. They explained the great signs and wonders that God had wrought among the Gentiles by them (see v. 12). After the crowd had again "held their peace," James reiterated Peter's teaching by saying: "Men, brethren, hear me. Simon hath related how God first visited to take of the Gentiles a people to his name. And to this agree the words of the prophets, as it is written: After these things I will return, and will rebuild the tabernacle of David, which is fallen down; and the ruins thereof I will rebuild, and I will set it up" (vv. 13-16).

After submitting to Peter and citing the Old Testament Scriptures in support of Peter's doctrinal decision,[32] James added a pas-

---

[32] James quoted from Amos 9:11-12; Jer 12:15; Is 45:21.

toral suggestion — namely, that the Gentiles should follow the universal, natural laws that God gave Noah: "For which cause I judge that they, who from among the Gentiles are converted to God, are not to be disquieted. But that we write unto them, that they refrain themselves from the pollutions of idols, and from fornication, and from things strangled, and from blood" (vv. 19-20).

First, notice that neither Peter nor any apostle used a *sola Scriptura* approach to resolve the issue. Peter didn't even refer to Scripture when rendering his decision. In fact, if the Church had used the Scriptures alone to resolve the question, the decision would have been quite different. All of the patriarchs and prophets were circumcised, the apostles were circumcised, and even Jesus was circumcised. At this point in time, there was nothing in Scripture that rescinded the circumcision requirement. Instead, based on an *oral* teaching of Christ, which He had handed on to His apostles (which the Church calls "Tradition"), Peter determined that circumcision no longer applied. Peter "loosed" the circumcision requirement, and "bound" the entire Church to his teaching.

Second, we address the effect that Peter's decision had on the assembly. We recall that after Peter spoke, "all the multitude held their peace" (v. 12). The Greek word for "*held their peace*" (*esigese*) comes from the verb *sigao*, which means "be silent." Some non-Catholics try to downplay Peter's authority by saying that the "silence" in verse 12 was not caused by Peter, but was brought about in preparation for Paul and Barnabas' teaching. In so doing, the argument overlooks all the biblical precedent for Peter's authority in the previous chapters of the Acts of the Apostles and elsewhere. Nevertheless, let's take a look at the argument.

Greek verbs use several tenses to describe actions that occurred in the past. For example, the perfect tense refers to an action in the past that has been completed, but its effects are still experienced in the future. The imperfect tense refers to an action in the past that was ongoing in the past. The aorist tense describes an action in the past that has ceased. The aorist tense does not describe the effects that the action may have on the future.

In this case, *esigese* is the aorist tense. This means that it points to an action in the past that has ceased. As applied here, the "multitude holding their peace" was caused by an action in the past — namely, Peter's speech, which now had ceased. It cannot point to Paul and Barnabas' speech because their speech was a future action, and aorist tenses do not describe future actions. In addition, Paul and Barnabas only spoke of the signs and wonders with which God had blessed the Gentiles, but did not give the Church any definitive teaching. The silence was brought about by Peter's colossal decision, not the supporting statements of Paul and Barnabas.

We see a similar application of the verb *sigao* in verse 13, after Paul and Barnabas had finished speaking and James entered the fray: "And after *they had held their peace*, James answered, saying: Men, brethren, hear me" (v. 13). The Greek verb for "they had held their peace" (*sigesai*) is also the aorist tense, and simply means "after they had finished speaking." This usage means that James did not speak until Paul and Barnabas were finished. It does not mean that James caused the silence during his speech. James received the silence caused by Paul and Barnabas, just as Paul and Barnabas received the silence caused by Peter. In fact, Peter was the one who *initially* caused *all* the silence, since there was "much disputing" until Peter "rose up" to issue his decision. Paul, Barnabas, and James were mere beneficiaries of the silence brought about by Peter's definitive teaching.

Didn't James Have the Final Word?

In another attempt to diminish Peter's authority, some non-Catholics argue that James had the final word in resolving the issue. We just saw, in Acts 15, how James completed the discussion after Peter, Paul, and Barnabas spoke. They point to James' statement: "Men, brethren, *hear me*" (v. 13). They also point to James' concluding statement: "For which cause *I judge* that they . . . are not to be disquieted" (v. 19). Based on these statements, opponents of the papacy argue that James, and not Peter, is the one who is speaking authoritatively for the Church.

This argument has no merit at all. Luke introduces James' address by saying "James *answered*" (v. 13). The use of the Greek word for "answered" (*apekrithe*) means that James is simply responding to, and in this case, *endorsing* Peter's definitive teaching, not independently issuing a teaching of his own. James' own words support this conclusion. The first thing James does in introducing his comments is to *rely upon the authority of Peter*. He says: "*Simon* hath related how God first visited to take of the Gentiles a people to his name" (v. 14).

The other important fact is how James describes Peter's teaching. James says "Simon *hath related.* . . ." The Greek word for "hath related" is *exegesato*, which refers to a definitive declaration that requires obedience on the part of the listener. We see this same word in John 1:18, where Jesus declares the Father: "No man hath seen God at any time: the only begotten Son who is in the bosom of the Father, he hath *declared* him." Just as Jesus declares the Father's teaching, Peter declares Jesus' teaching. Thus, James views Peter's teaching as an authoritative declaration for the entire Church, and he submits to Peter's authority.

When James says, "Brethren, *hear me*," the use of the Greek word (*akouoo*) simply means "I would like your attention." We see the same word in the immediately preceding verse, where it says "and they *heard* Barnabas and Paul" (v. 12). It is a common word that does not necessarily imply any kind of authority, even when used in the imperative tense, as James does here. For example, James also uses the imperative tense of *akouoo* in his epistle: "*Hearken*, my dearest brethren: hath not God chosen the poor in this world, rich in faith, and heirs of the kingdom which God hath promised to them that love him?" (Jas 2:5). In this case, James is not issuing a dogmatic teaching; he is only asking a rhetorical question regarding how God chooses the poor in the world to be rich in faith.

By saying "hear me," James is simply trying to maintain the crowds' attention, not prepare them for a dogmatic decree. Peter has already settled the issue, which James acknowledges by citing Peter as his primary authority (see v. 14). Because the issue is settled, James wants to ensure that he will still have a chance to follow up with some pastoral advice in support of Peter's dogmatic teaching. This pastoral advice concerns the application of the covenant laws God gave to Noah after the flood.[33] James says that the Gentiles should "refrain themselves from the pollutions of idols, and from fornication, and from things strangled, and from blood" (v. 20).

Thus, James fully supports Peter's definitive teaching that the Gentiles are not subject to the laws of circumcision. By proposing that the Gentiles follow the Noachide laws, James desires to facilitate their harmonious inclusion in the Church. These are laws that all just men follow, according to Jewish tradition. In other words, James believes that the Gentiles should follow certain rules that are consistent with Jewish law, so that they can get along with the Jews. James' advice is purely pastoral, and it reflects his Jewish perspective on Peter's definitive decision.

As we mentioned, non-Catholics also believe that James gave the definitive judgment at the council because he said: "For which cause *I judge . . .*" (v. 19). This, however, actually highlights that

---

[33] The Noachide laws were seven rules of morality that preceded the Torah (that is, they applied to all of humanity before there were "Jews" or "Gentiles"). These were: (1) employing a system of civil justice, and prohibitions on (2) blasphemy, (3) idolatry, (4) sexual immorality, (5) murder, (6) theft, and (7) eating flesh from a living animal.

James' statement was not authoritative. The Greek phrase for "I judge" (*ego krino*) simply means "it is my opinion."[34] It does not connote an authoritative decision, and certainly not in the context of an ecclesiastical declaration.

For example, elsewhere in Acts, Paul tells the jealous Jews that they "judge" (*krino*) themselves unworthy of eternal life (see Acts 13:46). This usage refers to the Jews' fallible opinions, not their authority over matters of faith and morals. Jesus also uses the identical phrase when He says, "I judge no one" (*ego krino*) in the context of not forming opinions about people based on misinformation. In using *ego krino*, James wishes to caveat his remarks by prefacing that he is merely expressing his feelings on the issue, not speaking authoritatively for the Church.

There is a final important point. James was the bishop of Jerusalem, where this first council took place. Yet not only did Peter speak *before* James, but Peter definitively settled the question *on his own*. No one questioned Peter's actions. This reminds us of Paul's fifteen-day visit with Peter, and not James, during his travels to Jerusalem (see Gal 1:18). Peter alone spoke on his own authority, resolved the issue, silenced the crowd, and received obedience. This further demonstrates that James was under the authority of Peter, not the other way around.

As all future councils would do, the Council of Jerusalem documented its proceedings with a letter to the entire Church and declared that the council was guided by the Holy Spirit (see Acts 15:23, 28). The pastoral initiatives set forth by the letter were followed for years to come. For example, Paul referred to the letter in Acts 21:25: "But as touching the Gentiles that believe, *we have written*, decreeing that they should only refrain themselves from that which has been offered to idols, and from blood, and from things strangled, and from fornication."

---

[34] See, for example, Acts 16:15; Rom 14:5; 1 Cor 7:37.

As more and more Gentiles came into the Church, Paul modified his pastoral approach. He allowed Christians to eat with unbelievers[35] and to eat meat sacrificed to idols,[36] so long as it did not scandalize fellow believers. However, Paul wrote more than any other apostle in support of Peter's dogmatic teaching about the uselessness of circumcision in the New Covenant.[37]

The differences between Peter's and James' roles at the Council of Jerusalem can be summarized as follows:

- Peter rises, speaks first, and quiets the disputing crowd / James speaks last and only in support of Peter's teaching (his affect on the crowd is not noted).
- Peter addresses a doctrinal issue / James addresses a pastoral issue.
- Peter renders a dogmatic decree / James merely gives his opinion.
- Peter is the leader of the council / James is an obedient bishop.

The Council of Jerusalem was a regional council held by the Church around A.D. 49. This council served as the blueprint for how the Church would conduct its future ecumenical councils over the centuries (the Church has had twenty-one ecumenical councils to date, the last being the Second Vatican Council, 1962-1965). The Council of Jerusalem displays the same features as the later Church councils. For example:

- It is a meeting of the entire Church.
- It addresses questions of faith or morals.

---

[35] See 1 Cor 10:25-30.
[36] See 1 Cor 8:7-13.
[37] Rom 2:25-29; 3:1, 30; 4:9-12; 1 Cor 7:19; Gal 5:6; 6:15; Phil 3:3; Col 2:11; 3:11; Tit 1:10.

- It sets forth teachings that are binding on the entire Church.
- It records its decrees in a written document for the entire Church.
- It declares that its decrees have been guided by the Holy Spirit.
- The pope presides over the council and approves its decisions in order for the council to take effect.

CHAPTER SEVEN

—⌘—

Peter and Apostolic Succession

The biblical basis for Peter's unique role in the early Church is without serious question. Many non-Catholics would even agree. The real question for opponents of the papacy is not about Peter's authority per se. Instead, the question is whether or not Jesus intended to continue Peter's ministry through a line of successors after Peter died. If He did, then the Catholic Church is the only institution to satisfy that criterion.

From a historical perspective, the unbroken lineage of papal successors is well-documented. In the Appendix, we list all of the 264 successors to Peter throughout the history of the Church. After Peter died, the keys to the kingdom of heaven were passed to Linus, then Anacletus, then Clement, then Evaristus, and so on, all the way down to our current Holy Father.

Thus, the early Christians interpreted Christ's Word to mandate a plan of succession, and that is exactly what they implemented. They recognized that Jesus would need a steward over His kingdom throughout the ages until He came again. This raises many thought-provoking questions. For example, did these Christians, who were closest to Christ and the apostles, totally miss the boat by implementing such a plan? Are the 264 successors to Peter over the last twenty centuries part of one big misunderstanding? Is the longest-reigning kingdom in the history of the civilized world of no divine significance?

From a logical perspective, it would not make any sense for Jesus to give the Church the divine leadership of Peter during her first thirty years of existence and then take it away after Peter died. That would be like the founding fathers of our country eliminating the office of the presidency after George Washington died. Imagine them saying, "Now that Washington is dead, we will be governed solely by the Constitution!" Isn't this far-fetched hypothetical analogous to "Bible" Christians who declare that the Bible is our only authority? If our country needs a leader, how much more would the worldwide family of God need a leader?

If Jesus needed Peter to guide the Church for the first three decades, He would need someone else to assume Peter's leadership after Peter was martyred. After all, Peter's work was not finished in A.D. 67. The Church was still a mustard seed. She was heeding Christ's mandate to "preach the gospel to all nations" by waging spiritual battle amidst bloody persecutions. While Peter got the Church "off the ground," the road to evangelization had only just begun. Hers was a formidable task that would require ongoing leadership and divine protection.

This is why Jesus gave Peter "the keys to the kingdom of heaven." The keys would serve two purposes: (1) to delegate to Peter supreme authority over the Church and (2) to facilitate a plan of succession to Peter's ministry. In this way, the Church would have one leader who would speak for Jesus Christ until Christ came in judgment at the end of the world. This singular office of Peter would ensure the integrity of the Gospel message and the unity of God's New Covenant family throughout the ages. The passing of the keys would also prevent the gates of hell from prevailing against the Church until Christ's Second Coming.

The Keys and Succession

How can we be sure that Peter's "keys" point to an office with succession? By looking at Scripture. Other than Matthew 16:19, the only time Scripture mentions "keys" in the context of a "kingdom" is when it describes the *succession to* the office of chief steward in the Davidic kingdom. As we have seen, this occurs in Isaiah 22, where God appoints Eliakim to succeed to Shebna's office by the passing of the key (v. 22). God not only uses the key as a symbol of authority, *but also to facilitate dynastic succession.*

At the time of Eliakim's appointment, the keys had facilitated the succession of chief stewards for three centuries. When the steward died, his office did not. The key survived the key-holder, and it was given to the next steward in charge of the kingdom. As we have seen, Ahishar was the chief steward under Solomon;[1] Arza served under Elah;[2] Obadiah was over the house of Ahab;[3] an unnamed steward was over the house of Joram;[4] and Azrikam served under Maaseiah.[5] The continuity of stewards was preserved by the passing of the keys.

If the "keys" were used to facilitate a succession of stewards in the Old Covenant kingdom, why wouldn't they do the same thing in the New Covenant kingdom? Isn't this especially compelling considering that Jesus, the Son of David, came to restore the very Davidic kingdom that was preserved through the passing of the keys? Non-Catholics want to divest the keys of any notion of succession, but Scripture says precisely the opposite.

The similarities between Eliakim and Peter further establish the connection between the Old and New Covenant kingdoms. Both Eliakim and Peter were stewards of a kingdom; both served and were second only to the king; both had the keys to the kingdom; both had the authority to bind (shut) and loose (open); both were called father (papa) to God's people; both were fastened

---

[1] 3 Kings 4:6 (1 Kings in RSV-CE).
[2] 3 Kings 16:9.
[3] 3 Kings 18:3.
[4] 4 Kings 10:5 (2 Kings in RSV-CE).
[5] 2 Para 28:7 (2 Chron in RSV-CE).

in a sure place (rock); *and both had successors*. If we let Scripture interpret Scripture, we must conclude that the keys in the New Covenant serve the same objectives as they did in the Old Covenant: to vest with authority *and facilitate succession*.

While Protestants believe that Christians are governed by the Bible alone, kingdoms are not governed by books. They are governed by leaders to whom authority is due. Jesus assigns His kingdom to the apostles and their successors, not to a book that wouldn't be compiled for three centuries.[6] If kingdoms are to endure, they must have a visible leader and a plan for succession because their leaders won't live forever (on earth). Where there is authority, there must also be a means to *preserve* that authority. Otherwise, the authority serves no enduring purpose.

Jesus repeatedly describes the Church as the "kingdom of heaven." When the king is absent, Scripture teaches that the chief steward serves in his place. He exercises the king's own authority by delegation. Since Christ our King is in heaven, He rules over His kingdom-Church through a succession of Vicars on earth. When one Vicar dies or becomes incapable of serving, the keys are passed to the next man He chooses. The keys both delegate and preserve the authority that God has gifted His Vicar to run the kingdom. Then, when Christ comes again, He will reclaim the keys to His kingdom and judge the living and the dead.

The Chair and Succession

The Old Testament practice of succession to an authoritative teaching office is also seen with Moses. We recall that Moses, like Peter, received a revelation from God while standing near a large rock formation. God then appointed Moses over His covenant people, and gave Moses the divine authority to interpret His Word and render binding judgments. Because Moses was the official teacher of

---

[6] See Lk 22:29-30; 12:32.

Israel, Moses' authority was symbolized by his "chair." Moses would sit in this chair to judge the people and infallibly interpret the Word of God: "And the next day Moses sat, to judge the people, who stood by Moses from morning until night" (Ex 18:13).

By the time of Jesus' ministry, Moses' chair of authority had been preserved through priestly succession for two thousand years. Jesus acknowledged this seat of authority when He said: "The scribes and the Pharisees have sitten on the chair of Moses. All things therefore whatsoever they shall say to you, observe and do."[7] Those who succeeded to Moses' teaching office would sit in the "chair of Moses."

In Jesus' time, Caiaphas occupied this chair, prophesying infallibly about Jesus' death and binding the people to his judgments. Since Peter was the official teacher of the New Israel, the Church, his authority was also symbolized by his "chair," or "seat," or "throne." Peter's papal throne has also survived for almost two thousand years.

Scripture often refers to the "throne" when describing royal succession within the Davidic kingdom. For example:

- "And you shall come up after him, and he shall come, and shall sit upon my *throne*, and he shall reign in my stead: and I will appoint him to be ruler over Israel, and over Juda."[8]
- "And Solomon sat *upon the throne* of his father David, and his kingdom was strengthened exceedingly."[9]
- "This was the word of the Lord, which he spoke to Jehu, saying: Thy children to the fourth generation shall sit *upon the throne* of Israel."[10]

---

[7] Mt 23:2-3.
[8] 3 Kings 1:35; see also 3 Kings 1:46; 16:11.
[9] 3 Kings 2:12.
[10] 4 Kings 15:12.

- "The Lord hath sworn truth to David, and he will not make it void: of the fruit of thy womb I will set *upon thy throne*. If thy children will keep my covenant, and these my testimonies which I shall teach them: Their children also for evermore shall sit *upon thy throne*."[11]

Even in the ancient kingdom of Egypt, where Joseph was appointed vizier, there was a succession of stewards and kings "who would sit on the throne":

- "And all the first-born in the land of the Egypt shall die, from the first-born of Pharaoh who sits *upon his throne*, even to the first-born of the maidservant who is behind the mill, and all the first-born of the cattle."[12]
- "At midnight the LORD smote all the first-born in the land of Egypt, from the first-born of Pharaoh who sat *on his throne* to the firstborn of the captive who was in the dungeon, and all the firstborn of the cattle."[13]

These biblical precedents demonstrate that royal and priestly succession is attributed to the person with the "keys" and the one who sits on the "throne." The early Christians, steeped in such Semitic terminology and symbolism, equated these precedents with Peter and his successive ruling office within the Church. Peter was the Vicar of Christ the King, whose authority was represented by his chair and his keys. These symbols of authority would not die with Peter, but would be passed down through the ages to his successors. Peter's office, which would be filled by successors, flowed naturally from the Old Testament precedents that preceded it, and no one seriously questioned it until the Protestant Reformation.

---

[11] Ps 131(132):11-12.
[12] Ex 11:5 (RSV-CE)
[13] Ex 12:29 (RSV-CE).

The Apostles and Succession

In addition to appointing successors to the chair of Peter, God also calls men to succeed to the office of the apostles as bishops, priests, and deacons. In this way, the Gospel of Jesus Christ can be spread not only from generation to generation, but from jurisdiction to jurisdiction as well. References to these offices within the Church are found throughout the Scriptures. For example, Paul writes elsewhere that Christ's Church has bishops (in Greek, *episkopoi*)[14] who serve in a particular location, priests (in Greek, *presbuteroi*)[15] who serve the bishops, and deacons (in Greek, *diakonoi*)[16] who assist the priests and serve the entire community.

The New Testament structure of the Church is based upon the Old Testament hierarchies of priestly and royal authority that God established in the Mosaic and Davidic covenants. This makes sense because God is the single source of all these revelations. God builds upon His revelations over time. Scripture interprets Scripture. What God revealed in the Old is fulfilled in the New. Just as God chose a vicar in the Old Covenant (Moses), He also chooses one in the New (Peter). Similarly, just as God established a religious hierarchy in the Old, He does the same in the New.

Scripture says Moses "appointed them rulers of the people, rulers over thousands, and over hundreds, and over fifties, and over tens. And they judged the people at all times: and whatsoever was of greater difficulty they referred to him, and they judged the easier cases only."[17] In the Old Covenant, God's vicar Moses appointed leaders to serve under him. It is no surprise that Peter, God's Vicar in the New Covenant, is the first person to do the very same thing.

---

[14] See Acts 20:28; Phil 1:1; Tit 1:7.
[15] See Acts 20:17; Tit 1:5; 1 Tim 5:17; Jas 5:14.
[16] Phil 1:1; 1 Tim 3:8
[17] Ex 18:25-26.

We recall how Peter directed the succession of Matthias to Judas Iscariot's apostolic office, notwithstanding Judas' terrible sin of betraying the Lord. Implementing a succession plan was Peter's first order of business. In interpreting the Psalms, Peter bound the Church to his first infallible judgment when he declared:

> For it is written in the book of Psalms: Let their habitation become desolate, and let there be none to dwell therein. And his *bishopric* let another take. Wherefore of these men who have companied with us all the time that the Lord Jesus came in and went out among us, beginning from the baptism of John, until the day wherein he was taken up from us, one of these must be *made* a witness with us of his resurrection.[18]

Peter's declaration shows the importance he gave to apostolic succession. In verse 20, Peter used the Greek word *episkopee* for "bishopric." This word describes the *office* to which the person is succeeding, and *not* the person himself. For example, Paul used the same word to describe the "office of bishop" in his first letter to Timothy: "If a man desire the *office of a bishop*, he desireth a good work."[19] This demonstrates that Peter, in interpreting the Psalms, was placing foremost importance upon the *succession to the office of bishop* (not the officeholder). This raises another obvious question: If Peter wanted a successor to Judas Iscariot, isn't it reasonable to conclude he wanted a successor to his office as well?

Thus, the word *episkopee* refers to an ecclesiastical office, and not to the person holding the office. If Peter wished to emphasize the officeholder, he would have used another word, *episkopos*. Paul's letter to Timothy demonstrates this distinction. Immedi-

---

[18] Acts 1:20-22.
[19] 1 Tim 3:1.

ately after Paul refers to the *episkopee* (office of bishop), he says an *episkopos* (person of bishop) "must be above reproach."[20] Peter's use of *episkopee* also demonstrates that succession applies to bishops, and not to apostles only, as some non-Catholics contend. Peter's teaching is clear: A bishop holds an office, and when he dies, his office must be filled with a successor.

This New Testament hierarchy within the Church naturally replaced the Old Testament hierarchy of the Sanhedrin. This visible and authoritative body is also consistent with Jesus' use of *ecclesia* to describe the Church that He builds upon Peter. We have seen that *ecclesia* refers to a formal, hierarchical assembly with visible leadership and authority. This hierarchy is present within the Catholic Church's two-thousand-year-old structure of popes, bishops, priests, and deacons.

Through this structure, Christ could promise His apostles (whom He knew would die) that He would be with them "all days, even to the consummation of the world" (Mt 28:20). This ecclesiastical structure, which is clearly rooted in Scripture, contravenes the common Protestant belief that "church" is an invisible association of believers loosely connected by their faith in the Bible alone.

The "Laying on of Hands"

How does a bishop succeed to the office? The same way that Moses' leaders succeeded to their offices: By the ceremonial rite of the "laying on of hands." Scripture explains how God directed Moses to implement His succession plan by laying his hands upon Joshua, thereby investing him with divine authority:

- "And the LORD said to Moses, 'Take Joshua the son of Nun, a man in whom is the spirit, and *lay your hand upon*

---

[20] 1 Tim 3:2 (RSV-CE).

him. . . . You shall invest him with some of your authority,
that all the congregation of the people of Israel may
obey."[21]

- "And Moses did as the LORD commanded him; he took
Joshua and caused him to stand before Eleazar the priest
and the whole congregation, and *he laid his hands upon
him*, and commissioned him as the LORD directed through
Moses."[22]

- "And Joshua the son of Nun was full of the spirit of wisdom, for Moses *had laid his hands upon him*; so the people of Israel obeyed him, and did as the LORD had
commanded Moses."[23]

This rite of succession, which was implemented by God Himself, ensured a legitimate transfer of priestly authority from one
generation to the next. The act of laying hands created an unin-
terrupted lineage of successors. This lineage could be traced all the
way back to Moses, the original authority-holder, who was
appointed directly by God. Anyone who was not so formally commissioned had no authority.[24] We saw this with Korah in the Old
Testament and Simon in the New Testament.[25] Both men sought
to be religious leaders without being appointed through the laying on of hands, and both were punished for their wickedness.

Since God implemented the laying on of hands in the Old
Testament, can it be any surprise that the Church implemented
succession the same way? Not at all. While God changed the leadership (from the Sanhedrin to the apostles), He kept the appointment process the same. He builds upon His revelation.

---

[21] Num 27:18, 20 (RSV-CE).
[22] Num 27:22-23 (RSV-CE).
[23] Dt 34:9 (RSV-CE).
[24] See, for example, Num 16:40.
[25] See Num 16 and Acts 8.

When Peter directs the succession of Matthias to Judas' office, which is the *first* instance of apostolic succession in the New Testament, he says that "one of these must be *made* a witness with us of his resurrection" (Acts 1:22). The Greek verb for "made" is *genesthai*, which literally means "ordained." This is another way to describe being "made" a priest through the laying on of hands. Christ instituted priestly ordination as one of the seven sacraments of His Catholic Church, which is also known as holy orders.

For example, in the Acts of the Apostles, we read the following:

- "And what they said pleased the whole multitude, and they chose Stephen, a man full of faith and of the Holy Spirit, and Philip, and Prochorus, and Nicanor, and Timon, and Parmenas, and Nicolaus, a proselyte of Antioch. These they set before the apostles, and they prayed and *laid their hands upon them*."[26]
- "While they were worshiping the Lord and fasting, the Holy Spirit said, 'Set apart for me Barnabas and Saul for the work to which I have called them.' Then after fasting and praying *they laid their hands on them* and sent them off."[27]
- "And when they *had ordained to them priests* in every church, and had prayed with fasting, they commended them to the Lord, in whom they believed."[28]

Paul also refers to the gift of the laying on of hands in his epistles. For example, Paul tells Timothy, (who was the bishop he had ordained to head the church at Ephesus):

---

[26] Acts 6:5-6 (RSV-CE)
[27] Acts 13:2-3 (RSV-CE)
[28] Acts 14:22.

- "Neglect not the grace that is in thee, which was given thee by prophesy, with *imposition of the hands* of the priesthood."[29]
- "*Impose not hands* lightly upon any man, neither be partaker of other men's sins. Keep thyself chaste."[30]
- "For which cause I admonish thee, that thou stir up the grace of God which is in thee, by the *imposition of my hands*."[31]

Paul also tells Titus: "For this cause I left thee in Crete, that thou shouldest set in order the things that are wanting, and shouldest *ordain priests* in every city, as I also appointed thee."[32]

Like the priesthood of the Old Covenant, the priesthood of the New Covenant is brought about by the imposition of hands from one who is in authority. Because the Catholic Church is the Church of the New Testament, all of her bishops, priests, and deacons can trace their ordinations back to the original apostles through the laying on of hands. This means that they can trace their authority to Christ Himself. Protestant pastors can make no such claim.

If the laying on of hands does not come from someone who has legitimate authority to begin with, there is no authority to transfer. Not just anybody can claim to possess the keys of the kingdom of heaven (only Peter and his successors can do so). Further, not just anybody can claim to share in the power of the keys (only those with apostolic succession can do so). It is only those united to Christ and His Vicar who can share in Christ's priestly power, and this comes about only through apostolic ordination, or holy orders.

Of course, if anyone could lay hands on anyone else, the rite of ordination would be meaningless. Anyone could infiltrate the

[29] 1 Tim 4:14.
[30] 1 Tim 5:22.
[31] 2 Tim 1:6.
[32] Tit 1:5.

Church and cause spiritual havoc. But God does not implement meaningless rites. Through the laying on of hands, God ensures us a legitimate body of teaching authority, and He provides a mechanism that attempts to thwart the proliferation of false teachers in the Church. After Paul exhorts the bishops to rule the Church, he warns them: "I know that, after my departure, ravening wolves will enter in among you, not sparing the flock."[33] The preservation of apostolic succession through the laying on of hands keeps these false teachers out of Christ's true Church.

The Scriptures also teach us that *God Himself* calls men to holy orders through the intercession of the Church. After prayer and fasting, the Church makes a binding decision about whom to ordain, and this decision is ratified by God in eternity. This is part of the Church's binding and loosing authority, where heaven collaborates with earth. For example, God reveals through Paul:

- "Take heed to yourselves, and to the whole flock, *wherein the [Holy Spirit] hath placed you bishops*, to *rule* the church of God, which he hath purchased with his own blood."[34]
- "Now he that confirmeth us with you in Christ, and *that hath anointed us, is God: Who also hath sealed us*, and given the pledge of the Spirit in our hearts."[35]
- "For if also I should boast somewhat more of our power, which *the Lord hath given us unto edification*, and not for your destruction, I should not be ashamed."[36]
- "Let a man so account of us as of the *ministers of Christ*, and the dispensers of the *mysteries of God*."[37]

---

[33] Acts 20:29.
[34] Acts 20:28.
[35] 2 Cor 1:21-22.
[36] 2 Cor 10:8.
[37] 1 Cor 4:1.

Where did the sacred writers learn that they were directly appointed by God? From our Lord Himself. Jesus teaches that His priests share His very own authority over the Church:

- "He that receiveth you, receiveth me: and he that receiveth me, receiveth him that sent me."[38]
- "Amen, amen I say to you, he that receiveth whomsoever I send, receiveth me; and he that receiveth me, receiveth him that sent me."[39]
- "He that heareth you, heareth me; and he that despiseth you, despiseth me; and he that despiseth me, despiseth him that sent me."[40]

If we accept those whom God calls through holy orders, we accept Jesus Christ. If we reject them, we reject Christ. This is part of the mystery of the Incarnation. God took on our humanity in Christ Jesus so that we could partake of His divinity for all eternity. This mystery of *Emmanuel* ("God with us") is made manifest through the priesthood. What the Father has given to Jesus, Jesus has given to His priests. This includes a share in the authority that Jesus exercises over heaven and earth.[41] Jesus says: "As thou hast sent me into the world, I also have sent them into the world" (Jn 17:18). To be true followers of Jesus and faithful to Scripture, we must submit ourselves to those He has appointed over us.

Priest Versus Elder

Speaking of the Catholic priesthood, many inquire about the difference, if any, between the terms "priest" and "elder." This is an important inquiry, because Protestants attempt to create a distinction between these titles in an effort to deny the Catholic

---

[38] Mt 10:40.
[39] Jn 13:20.
[40] Lk 10:16.
[41] See Mt 28:18.

priesthood. The Latin Vulgate translates the Greek word *presbuteros* into *presbyter*, which means "priest." The Rhemish New Testament translation of the Latin Vulgate confirms this by translating the Latin *presbyter* into "priest." The Old English version of the Rheims' translation uses the word "preost." The root word of *presbuteros* comes from the Greek word *presbus*, which means "old man" or "elder." Thus, in the early Church, the terms "priest" and "elder" were synonymous.

Many Protestant-English translations of the New Testament that came out after the Rheims translation of 1582 (like the King James Version of 1611) invariably substitute "elder" in place of "priest" when referring to the leaders of the New Testament Church.[42] While this would have made no difference to a first-century Christian (assuming, of course, the English language existed), Protestants try to redefine "elder" by divesting it of its priestly characteristics. They argue that an "elder" is simply someone whom a congregation chooses to lead a church. They must so argue, since they deny that Catholic priests forgive sins and offer the sacrifice of Christ in the Eucharist. Forgiving sins and offering sacrifice are the principal duties of a priest, and so priests cannot be a part of Protestant congregations.

One of many examples of this substitution is found in James 5:14-15, which describes the Church's sacrament of the anointing of the sick (also called "extreme unction"). The Douay-Rheims translates James 5:14 as follows:

> Is any man sick among you? Let him bring in the *priests* of the church, and let them pray over him, anointing him with oil in the name of the Lord.

---

[42] Interestingly, the Protestant translations such as the King James Version generally continue to use "priest" in their Old Testament translations (there are over 1,100 such examples), as well as when referring to the Mosaic priesthood in the New Testament.

The King James Version says:

Is any sick among you? Let him call for the *elders* of the church; and let them pray over him, anointing him with oil in the name of the Lord.

James 5:14 is a target for such a substitution because of what James says in the next verse (here, the King James Version): "And the prayer of faith shall save the sick, and the Lord shall raise him up; and if he have committed sins, *they shall be forgiven him*." Because verse 15 explicitly says that the prayers of the priests will forgive the sick man's sins, Protestants want to divest the text of any reference to "priests."

Why? They know that Jesus is our High *Priest* who forgives our sins. They also know that the Old Testament *priests* made atonement for people's sins.[43] If the Church of the Bible *also* has priests who forgive and atone for sins, it starts looking to them like the Catholic Church. Since Jesus is never described as an "elder," calling the Church leaders "elders," in their view, distinguishes the elders' work from the priestly work of Christ, such as forgiving sins. In this way, they can attribute the action of forgiving sins solely to God, and not to "priests" through whom God acts. This gives them a psychological comfort zone, and keeps their non-sacramental, Bible-alone theology in tact.

Protestants who try to distinguish between "elders" and "priests" also do not explain why their ecclesial communities generally do not have "bishops" or "deacons" like the Church of the Bible (as even their Protestant translations provide).[44] Nor do they explain why their "elders" do not have apostolic succession. Can

---

[43] See Lev 5:5-6.

[44] Protestant translations also replace the word "bishop" with the more generic word "overseer" (compare, for example, the King James translation of Acts 20:28 with that of the Douay-Rheims). This, again, is an attempt to downplay the hierarchical and apostolic nature of the Church.

they really trace their "ordinations" back to the apostles? How can their "churches" be the one Jesus builds on Peter if they don't have these biblical characteristics? How also can they explain their lack of unity on even the most basic doctrines of the Christian faith, such as baptism? Distinguishing "elders" from "priests" is a pure anachronism that is not supported by the historical or etymological development of the original languages.

In fact, many Protestant translations demonstrate that there is no distinction between "elders" and "priests." Their most hallowed translation, the King James Version, is a good example. In chapter five of the Apocalypse (Revelation), it says that "the four beasts and four and twenty *elders* [in Greek, *presbuteroi*] fell down before the Lamb, having every one of them harps, and golden vials full of odours, which are the prayers of saints" (v. 8). Two verses later, the "elders" are called "priests": "And hast made us unto our God kings and *priests* [in Greek, *presbuteroi*]: and we shall reign on the earth" (v. 10).[45] In this passage, which describes the liturgical worship of Christ in heaven, there is no distinction between "elders" and "priests." The terms refer to the same people in heaven.

The elders are called "priests" because they are performing the *priestly* duty of offering incense before the throne of God. This is precisely what the Old Testament priests did as part of their liturgical worship. For example, in addition to sacrificing animals and atoning for sins, God repeatedly commanded Moses' priests to offer incense in golden vials at the altar. God's required offering was: "One spoon of gold of ten shekels, full of incense."[46] Therefore, the attempt to distinguish "elder" from "priest" is completely without merit.[47] It is nothing more than "incense" and mirrors.

---

[45] See also Apoc 1:6; 20:6 (Rev in RSV-CE).

[46] Num 7:20; also see Num 7:26, 32, 38, 44, 50, 56, 62, 68, 74, 80, 86 (King James Version).

[47] The King James Version properly translates 1 Pet 2:5, 9, where Peter says that the people of God are a "holy priesthood" and a "royal priesthood," respectively.

Closing

We close this chapter by reminding all Christians not to lose faith in the Church's teaching authority because her leaders are sinners. This is especially difficult today, where scandal in the Church is pervasive. But since the beginning of her divine institution, the Church has always been full of sinners. Christ's appointment of Judas Iscariot should remind us how sinful bishops can be. God did not say, "Obey your leaders and submit to them, but only if they remain sinless."[48] He says: "Obey your prelates, and be subject to them. For they watch as being to render an account of your souls" (Heb 13:17).

God warns us that the leaders of the Church, who are caretakers of our souls, might be unfaithful.[49] But unfaithful members do not nullify the faithfulness of God.[50] Paul says, "If we believe not, he continueth faithful, he can not deny himself."[51] Jesus says that the Church is like a net that catches fish of every kind, both good and bad.[52] God's mysterious plan for the Church requires the wheat and the chaff to remain side by side until the end of time.[53] Paul further says that a great house contains not only vessels of gold and silver, but also wood and earthenware; some for noble use and some for ignoble use.[54]

God does not guarantee that the leaders of the Church will be sinless. But He *does* guarantee that the gates of hell will not prevail against His Church. The gates of hell refer to the powers that lead those away from the truth. This means that the Church's *teaching office* (also called the Magisterium) is immune from teach-

---

[48] See Heb 13:17
[49] See 1 Tim 5:19.
[50] See Rom 3:3-4.
[51] 2 Tim 2:13.
[52] See Mt 13:47-50.
[53] See Mt 13:24-30.
[54] 2 Tim 2:20; see also Jer 24:1-10.

ing error, beginning with the chair of Peter. If it weren't so immune, the faithful would be deceived by Satan and the gates of hell would prevail. This would make our Lord a liar, and His sacrifice inefficacious. This, of course, is impossible.

The Church has survived in this world for almost two thousand years *because the papacy has survived*. The papacy has survived because Jesus has established it on the rock. Although the winds and floods and rains of the world have assailed her, she remains firmly established, never to be moved.[55] She will not cave in to the world because she is the spouse of the Lord Jesus who "has overcome the world" (Jn 16:33). No mere human institution could have ever endured twenty centuries of heresies, wars, persecutions, and defections without being divinely established and protected by God Almighty.

Not only has the Catholic Church survived, but her teachings have been a light to the world. She is the one who defined the doctrines of the Trinity and Christology. She is the one who determined the canon of Scripture. She is the one who has preserved Christ's teachings on sexual morality, while Protestant communities have buckled in compromise. And she has done this amidst an immoral and divided world that has exchanged the truth of God for a lie (see Rom 1:25). What other institution can say the same? The Catholic Church's consistency and unity in doctrine and morals proves to the world that the Father has sent His Son.[56] The papacy is our link between Jesus and mankind, between time and eternity, between heaven and earth.

---

[55] See Mt 7:24-25.
[56] See Jn 17:21, 23.

CHAPTER EIGHT

———

What Did the Fathers Say?

Up to this point, we have used Scripture alone to explain and defend the Catholic Church's teaching on the papacy. We will now look at some of the writings of the earliest Christians on this topic. We often refer to these men as the early Church Fathers, because they are our spiritual fathers in the faith. They presided over the earliest councils, wrote the first commentaries on Sacred Scripture, and laid the groundwork for the Church's theology for future generations. Because they were closest to Jesus and the apostles, these men provide invaluable insights regarding the true, universal, apostolic teaching on the papacy.

Protestant Christians are often not familiar with the Fathers. Some avoid the writings of the Fathers altogether. This is because they base their faith on the Bible alone. They often dismiss the writings of the Fathers on the ground that they are "extra-biblical" tradition. But without realizing it, these Christians rely heavily on the patristic traditions themselves.

As we have seen, the canon of Scripture is a perfect example. So is our understanding of the Blessed Trinity, as well as our understanding of how one enters into a valid marriage. None of these teachings are expounded in Scripture, and yet they are accepted by Catholics and Protestants alike. They are a part of the Christian tradition that we have received from the Fathers. Both Catholics and Protestants follow extra-biblical traditions. The only real difference is that Catholics are aware that they do and Protestants are not.

Studying the Fathers raises some obvious questions. Why would someone seeking the truth about Christianity in the twenty-first century not want to learn what a notable first-, second-, or third-century Christian said about a particular teaching? Why would they instead wish to rely upon their pastors or even themselves in interpreting Scripture? While Protestants accuse Catholics of blindly obeying the teachings of the pope, they often make themselves or their pastors into "popes" of a different kind. This private-judgment theology has caused the thousands of different divisions within Protestant Christianity today.

The truth is that we cannot, on our own, know what every particular Scripture passage means with infallible certainty. Peter said that "no prophecy of scripture is made by private interpretation."[1] While a literal reading of Matthew 16:18-19 provides compelling proof for the Catholic position, Protestants believe that they have reasonable alternative explanations. So how do we know what Matthew 16:18-19 really means?

The only way to know definitively is to ask Matthew what he meant when he wrote Matthew 16:18-19. We obviously cannot do this because Matthew is deceased. But we *can* know what Matthew meant by studying the writings of those who were taught directly by Matthew or received Matthew's teaching from generations closest to him. These are the early Church Fathers. They were closest to the apostles and the original transmission of the Gospel message. In interpreting Scripture, studying the Fathers is the next best thing to speaking with the authors of the Bible themselves.

One of the earliest quotes from the Fathers, which is also one of my favorites, comes from Ignatius. He was the bishop of Antioch, a thriving community of Gentile converts in the early Church. The Acts of the Apostles mentions Antioch quite frequently. Early Christian writers say that Ignatius was ordained by Peter, and was also the auditor of the Apostle John.

---

[1] 2 Pet 1:20.

The church in Antioch was fervent in the faith, and its members wanted to identify themselves as followers of Jesus. They wanted to separate themselves from the Judaic and pagan religiosity of their time. Therefore, the faithful of the church in Antioch began calling themselves "Christians." Luke mentions this historical fact in Acts 11:26: "At Antioch the disciples were first named Christians."

Because the members of the church in Antioch first called themselves "Christians," it is no surprise that they were the first to call themselves "Catholics" as well. Ignatius describes the Church as the "Catholic Church" in a letter he wrote on his way to martyrdom in A.D. 107. Since the Apostle John was exiled in Patmos at the end of the first century, this letter could have been written during his lifetime. The letter was also written during the reign of Pope Alexander I, the fifth successor to Peter. Ignatius writes:

> All of you, obey your bishops as Jesus Christ obeyed the Father, and obey the priesthood as you would the Apostles. Reverence the deacons also, as God commands. Apart from the bishop, let no one do anything of what pertains to the Church. The only true Eucharist is the one performed by the bishop or by him whom the bishop has appointed. Wherever the bishop is, there must be the congregation, just as wherever Jesus Christ is, there is the Catholic Church. (*Letter to the Smyrnaeans*, 8, 1)

We find these and many other descriptions of the infant Church by studying the Fathers. Since you have already heard from me, I will let the Fathers speak the rest of the way. The following are quotes from the Fathers during the first five hundred years of the Church, with no further commentary. Their writings describe the early Christians' understanding of the office of Peter, the keys, the chair, binding and loosing, infallibility, the primacy of Rome and other topics that we have covered in this book. They had a Catholic understanding because they were members of the Catholic Church.

It is interesting to note that there is not one single Father *who denied the Catholic understanding of the papacy.* This should alarm any non-Catholic who does. The Church teaches that where the Fathers have a unanimous interpretation of Scripture, Christians are not free to depart from their interpretation. Their unanimity demonstrates that the interpretation is part of the Sacred Tradition handed down to them by the apostles. This is the Tradition that Paul refers to throughout Scripture.[2]

Please keep in mind that this material only scratches the surface. There were more than one hundred Fathers of note who wrote extensive commentaries on Scripture, and we have selected only a few of them for this short chapter. Further, for every single quote provided, there are often a dozen or more to study. Our purpose is to provide a brief introduction to the Fathers, and to demonstrate that this book merely echoes their teachings.

Peter Is the Head of the Apostles

"It was His pleasure to communicate to the most highly esteemed of his disciples, in a peculiar manner, a name (Peter) drawn from the figures of Himself."   — TERTULLIAN, C. A.D. 200-220

"Peter, the Prince of the Apostles." — ORIGEN, C. A.D. 230-250

"Peter, the leader and prince of the Apostles."
                                        — AUCTOR DE REBAPTISMATE, A.D. 254

"Peter, set above the apostles."
                              — PETER, BISHOP OF ALEXANDRIA, C. A.D. 306-311

---

[2] See, for example, 1 Cor 11:2; 2 Thess 2:15; 3:6. See also 1 Tim 6:20; 2 Tim 2:2; 3:14.

"That powerful and great one of the Apostles, who, on account of his excellence, was the leader of all the rest."

— EUSEBIUS, A.D. 325

"[Peter] the Prince of the Apostles."

— ANTHONY OF EGYPT, A.D. 330

"The earliest of the Syrian fathers of importance is Aphraates, who . . . urges his listeners to imitate Simon . . . the chief of the disciples."   — APHRAATES THE PERSIAN SAGE, C. A.D. 336

"We hail you, Peter, the Tongue of the disciples; the Voice of the heralds; the Eye of the Apostles; the Keeper of heaven; the First-born of those that bear the keys."

— EPHRAEM THE SYRIAN, C. A.D. 350-370

"The Chief, Peter."   — ATHANASIUS, A.D. 362

"And all being silent (for it was beyond man to learn) Peter, the Foremost of the Apostles, and Chief Herald of the Church, not using language of his own finding, nor persuaded by human reasoning, but having his mind enlightened from the Father, says to Him, 'Thou art the Christ,' not simply that, but, 'the Son of the living God.' And a blessing follows the speech."

— CYRIL OF JERUSALEM, C. A.D. 363

"Blessed Peter, to whom after his denial, it were enough if he obtained pardon, merited both to be prefigured before all the Apostles, and he alone received of the kingdom of heaven the keys to be communicated to the others. . . . The Head of the Apostles could so have governed himself as not to incur a crime of which he would have to repent."

— OPTATUS OF MILEVIS, C. A.D. 370

"Peter, the Chief of the disciples, but he was a Rock, not as a fisherman, but because full of zeal."
— GREGORY OF NAZIANZUS, A.D. 370

"The leader and coryphaeus of the Apostolic choir. . . . The head of the Apostles."   — GREGORY OF NYSSA, A.D. 371

"The Chief, Peter."   — MACARIUS OF EGYPT, A.D. 371

"[Peter,] Prince of the Apostles."   — FAUSTINUS, A.D. 383

"And the blessed Peter, who for a while denied the Lord, Peter who was the Chiefest of the Apostles, he who became unto us truly a firm Rock upon which is based the Lord's faith, upon which (Rock) the Church is in every way built."
— EPIPHANIUS, C. A.D. 385

"Peter, that Leader of the choir, that Mouth of the rest of the Apostles, that Head of the brotherhood, that One set over the entire universe, that Foundation of the Church."
— JOHN CHRYSOSTOM, C. A.D. 387

"Of this Church, Peter, the Apostle, on account of the Primacy of his Apostleship, bore a character which represented the whole Church. For as to what personally regards him, he was by nature but one man, by grace one Christian, by a more abundant grace, one, and that the First Apostle."   — AUGUSTINE, C. A.D. 400

"What has Paul to do with Aristotle? Or Peter with Plato? For as the latter [Plato] was the prince of philosophers, so was the former [Peter] chief of the Apostles; on him the Lord's Church was firmly founded, and neither rushing flood nor storm can shake it."
— JEROME, A.D. 417

"The institution of the universal nascent Church took its beginning from the honor of blessed Peter, in whom its government and
headship reside."   — POPE BONIFACE I, A.D. 420

"Peter, into whose person the power of all priests is gathered
together."   — ZACCHAEUS, A.D. 421

". . . Peter obtained his name from a Rock, because he was the First,
that merited to found the Church by the firmness of his faith. . . . Let
Peter hold his long-established Princedom (*principatum*) over the
Apostolic Choir; let him open the kingdom of heaven for those who
enter in; let him with power bind the guilty, with clemency absolve
the penitent."   — PETER CHRYSOLOGUS, A.D. 432

"Peter, the coryphaeus of the disciples, and the one set over (or the
chief of) the Apostles."   — PROCLUS, C. A.D. 434

"Behold, that succor is given to a penitent Apostle, who is the
Bishop of bishops, and a greater rank is restored to him now
weeping than was taken from him when he 'denied.' "
                                           — ARNOBIUS JUNIOR, A.D. 440

"But the Lord willed the sacrament of this office (of the apostolic
trumpet) to pertain to all the Apostles in such manner, as that He
placed it principally in the blessed Peter, the Chief of all the Apostles, and wishes His gifts to flow unto the whole body, from him
(Peter) as from a Head; that whoso should dare withdraw from the
solidity of Peter, might know himself to be an alien from the
divine mystery."   — POPE LEO I, C. A.D. 440-461

"Likewise, for Basil, St. Peter is the leader (coryphaeus) of the
apostles, and the chief (*prostates*) of the disciples of Christ."
                                           —BASIL OF SELEUCIA, A.D. 448

"Peter, who was foremost in the choir of the Apostles, and always ruled among them."   — NILUS, A.D. 448

"There were assuredly twelve Apostles, endowed with equal merits and equal dignity; and whereas they all shone equally with spiritual light, yet was it Christ's will that One among them should be the Ruler (prince — *principem*), etc."
                                    — POPE GELASIUS I, A.D. 492

Peter Is the Rock of the Church

"Was anything hidden from Peter, who was called the Rock whereon the Church was to be built; who obtained the keys of the kingdom of heaven, and the power of loosing and of binding in heaven and on earth?"   — TERTULLIAN, C. A.D. 200-220

"Peter, the Rock of the faith, whom Christ our Lord called blessed, the teacher of the Church, the first disciple, he who has the keys of the kingdom."   — HIPPOLYTUS, C. A.D. 225

"See what is said by the Lord to [Peter], that great foundation of the Church, and most solid rock, upon which Christ founded the Church [Mt 16:18]. 'Oh you of little faith! Why did you doubt?' [Mt 14:31]."   — ORIGEN, C. A.D. 230-250

"God is one, and Christ is one, and the Church is one, and the Chair one, founded, by the Lord's word, upon a rock; another altar and a new priesthood, besides the one altar and the one priesthood, cannot be set up."   — CYPRIAN, C. A.D. 246

"You support the name of Peter with worthy fortitude; and upon this foundation and upon the strength of this rock I will place My edifice that shall stand for ever with everlasting walls."

— JUVENCUS, A.D. 326

"As soon as he offered to God contrition and penitence, and washed his sins in the tears of his grief, our Lord received him, and made him the Foundation, and called him the Rock of the edifice of the Church."   — JAMES OF NISIBIS, A.D. 340

"Simon my follower, I have made you the foundation of the holy Church [Mt 16:18]. I called you Peter, because you will support all its buildings. You are the inspector of those who will build on earth a Church for me. If they should wish to build what is false, you, the foundation, will condemn them. You are the head of the fountain from which My teaching flows, you are the chief of My disciples."   — EPHRAEM THE SYRIAN, C. A.D. 350-370

"He said to Peter, 'And upon this Rock I will build my Church, and the gates of hell shall not prevail against it."

— CYRIL OF JERUSALEM, A.D. 350

"Oh! In your designation by a new name, happy Foundation of the Church, and a Rock worthy of the building up of that which was to scatter the infernal laws, and the gates of hell, and all the bars of death!"   — HILARY OF POITIERS, A.D. 356

"See that of the disciples of Christ, all of whom were great and deserving of choice, one is called a Rock and is entrusted with the Foundations of the Church."

— GREGORY OF NAZIANZUS, A.D. 370

"The soul of the blessed Peter was called a lofty rock because he had a strong mooring in the faith and bore constantly and bravely the blows inflicted by temptations. All, therefore, who have acquired an understanding of the Godhead — on account of the breadth of mind and of those actions which proceed from it — are the peaks of mountains, and upon them the house of God is built."   — BASIL THE GREAT, A.D. 371

"The memory of Peter, the Head of the Apostles, is celebrated; and magnified indeed with him are the other members of the Church; but (upon him) is the Church of God firmly established. For he is, agreeably to the gift conferred upon him by the Lord, that unbroken and most firm Rock upon which the Lord built His Church."   — GREGORY OF NYSSA, A.D. 371

"The Lord spoke to one (Peter), that thus He might lay the foundation of unity from one."   — PACIAN, A.D. 372

"The Lord said to Peter: 'On this rock I will build my church'; that is, in this confession of catholic faith I will consolidate the faithful for life."   — AMBROSIASTER, C. A.D. 380-384

"Let it suffice that faults have to this point been committed in this matter; and now let the above-named rule be observed by all priests (Bishops) who do not wish to be rent from that solid Apostolic Rock upon which Christ constructed the Universal Church."
                          — Pope SIRICIUS, C. A.D. 384-386

"This was befitting in that First of the Apostles, that firm Rock upon which the Church of God is built, and 'the gates of hell shall not prevail against it.' 'The gates of hell' are heretics and heresiarchs."   — EPIPHANIUS, C. A.D. 385

"Peter is called 'rock' because, like an immovable rock, he sustains the joints and mass of the entire Christian edifice."
                          — AMBROSE, C. A.D. 385-389

" 'Thou art Peter, and upon this rock I will build my Church.' As He bestowed light on His Apostles, so that they were to be called 'light of the world,' and as they obtained other titles from the Lord, so also to Simon, who believed on the Rock Christ, was given the name Peter (Rock). And in accordance with the metaphor of a rock, it is justly said to him, 'I will build my Church on thee.' " — JEROME, C. A.D. 385-398

"This very Peter — and when I name Peter I name that unbroken Rock, that firm Foundation, the Great Apostle, the First of the disciples, the First called, and the First who obeyed."
— JOHN CHRYSOSTOM, C. A.D. 387

"Peter went not away unrequited and unrewarded; but, declared 'Blessed' by the truly blessed, he is called the rock of faith, and the foundation and substructure of the Church of God."
— ASTERIUS, A.D. 387

"For what the Church is essentially in Christ, such representatively is Peter in the rock (*petra*); and in this representation Christ is to be understood as the Rock, Peter as the Church."
— AUGUSTINE, C. A.D. 400

"To Simon he gave the name Peter [Rock], that the name may anticipate the event itself; because as Christ the Lord was about to build His Church on Peter — that is, on the unbroken and sound doctrine of Peter and his unshaken faith — therefore, in prophetic spirit does He call him Peter." — VICTOR OF ANTIOCH, A.D. 405

"Peter, upon which rock Christ built His Church."
— PAULUS OROSIUS, C. A.D. 414-419

"He suffers him no longer to be called Simon, exercising authority and rule over him already as having become His own. But by a title suitable to the thing, He changed his name into Peter, from the word *petra* (rock); for on him He was afterwards to found His Church."   — CYRIL OF ALEXANDRIA, A.D. 424

"On account of this confession, the blessed Apostle merited to hear from the mouth of the Lord, 'Thou art Peter, and upon this rock. . . .' That is, you are the First to confess Me on earth, and I will make you to have a perpetual Primacy in heaven, and in My kingdom. And what more just than that the Church should be built on him, who gives so mighty a Foundation to the Church."   — MAXIMUS OF TURIN, A.D. 424

"For 'thou art Peter'; that is, whereas I am the inviolable Rock; I that Chief Cornerstone; I who make both one (Eph 2:6), I the Foundation besides which no one can lay other, nevertheless you also are a Rock, because you are consolidated by My power, that what things are mine by My power, may be common to you by being made partaker of them with Me."   — POPE LEO I, A.D. 440-461

Peter Has the Keys of the Kingdom and the Authority to Bind and Loose

"For if you think heaven is still closed, remember that the Lord left here the keys thereof to Peter, and through him to the Church; which keys every one that is here questioned and confesses, shall carry with him."   — TERTULLIAN, C. A.D. 200-220

"For first to Peter, upon whom He built the Church, and from whom He appointed and showed that unity should spring, the

Lord gave this power that that should be in heaven which he should have loosed on earth." — Cyprian, c. A.D. 246

". . . who says remission of sins can be given in the synagogues of heretics, not abiding on the foundation of the one Church, which was once first established by Christ on a Rock, may hence be understood that to Peter alone Christ said, 'Whatsoever thou shalt bind . . .'; and again, in the Gospel, when Christ breathed on the Apostles alone, saying, 'Receive ye the Holy Spirit. . . .' The power, therefore, of forgiving sins, was given to the Apostles, and to the Churches which they, sent forth by Christ, founded, and to the bishops who, by vicarious ordination, have succeed to them."
— Firmilian, c. A.D. 254

"And Jesus handed over the keys to Simon, and ascended and returned to Him who had sent Him."
— Aphraates the Persian Sage, c. A.D. 336

"For Peter was there, who carries the keys of heaven."
— Cyril of Jerusalem, c. A.D. 350

"Let us consider what happened to Simon, thanks to his chastity, for [Jesus] made him the foundation of the Church and made him hold authority, made him the chief of the Apostles and gave him the keys of souls." — Ephraem the Syrian, c. A.D. 350-370

"O blessed Keeper of the gate of heaven, to whose disposal are delivered the keys of the entrance into eternity; whose judgment on earth is an authority prejudged in heaven, so that the things that are either loosed or bound on earth, acquire in heaven too a like state of settlement." — Hilary of Poitiers, A.D. 356

"Blessed Peter, to whom after his denial, it were enough if he obtained pardon, merited both to be preferred before all the Apostles, and he alone received of the kingdom of heaven the keys to be communicated to the others."

— OPTATUS OF MILEVIS, c. A.D. 370

"That unbroken rock, who had the key."

— GREGORY OF NAZIANZUS, A.D. 370

"And when he, the instrument of such and so great a judgment; he the minister of the so great wrath of God upon a sinner; that blessed Peter, who was preferred before all the disciples; who alone received a greater testimony and blessing than the rest; he to whom were entrusted the keys of the kingdom of heaven. . . ."

— BASIL THE GREAT, A.D. 371

"The first Apostle, to whom the Lord gave the keys of the kingdom of heaven."   — AMBROSIASTER, c. A.D. 380-384

"For in every way was the faith confirmed in him who received the keys of heaven; who looses on earth and binds in heaven. For in him are found all subtle questions of faith."

— EPIPHANIUS, c. A.D. 385

". . . to him were given the keys of heaven; so that to them indeed whose faith agreed with theirs, [that is], with what Peter recognized in his way, and with [that of] the others, [namely,] what he along with the others had heard from Christ, [by] baptizing them in the name of the Father, and of the Son, and of the Holy Spirit, would he open the doors to the Kingdom of God."

— DIDYMUS THE BLIND, A.D. 385

"Therefore where Peter is, there is the Church; where the Church is, there death is not, but life eternal; and therefore it was added, and 'the gates of hell shall not prevail against it,' and, 'I will give to thee the keys of the kingdom of heaven.' Blessed Peter, against whom the gates of hell prevailed not, nor were the gates of heaven closed against him; but who, on the contrary, destroyed the porches of hell and opened the heavenly places."

— AMBROSE, C. A.D. 385-389

"He receives, too, by promise, 'the keys of the kingdom,' and becomes the Lord of the gates thereof, so as to open them to whom he may choose, and to close them against those against whom they justly ought to be shut, — plainly against the defiled and profane, and the deniers of this confession, through which, as a careful guardian of the wealth of the Churches, he was appointed to preside over the entrances into the Kingdom."   — ASTERIUS, A.D. 387

"The Church therefore which is founded on Christ, received in Peter the keys of the kingdom of heaven from Him, that is, the power of binding and of loosing sins." — AUGUSTINE, C. A.D. 400

"We in a special manner are constrained by our charge, which regards all men, we on whom Christ has, in the Person of the holy Peter the Apostle, when He gave him the keys to open and to shut, imposed as a necessity to be engaged about all men."

— POPE CELESTINE I, C. A.D. 423

"What could be more religiously done, than that he should receive the 'keys of heaven,' he who revealed the Lord of the heavenly kingdom; inasmuch as he who opened to believers the gates of faith, the same would also open for them the gates of heaven."

—MAXIMUS OF TURIN, A.D. 424

"O Peter, Prince of the Apostles, it is just that you should teach us, since you were yourself taught by the Lord; and also that you should open to us the gate of which you have received the key. Keep out all those who are undermining the heavenly House; turn away those who are trying to enter through false caverns and unlawful gates since it is certain that no one can enter in at the gate of the kingdom except the one unto whom the key, placed by you in the churches, shall open it."   — JOHN CASSIAN, A.D. 430

"Let Peter hold his ancient primacy of the Apostolic choir. Let him open to those who enter the kingdom of heaven. Let him bind the guilty with his power and absolve the penitent in kindness."
                                        — PETER CHRYSOLOGUS, A.D. 432

"For he was ordained before the rest in such a way that from his being called the Rock, from his being pronounced the Foundation, from his being constituted the Doorkeeper of the kingdom of heaven, from his being set as the umpire to bind and loose, whose judgments shall retain their validity in heaven, from all these mystical titles we might know the nature of his association with Christ."   — POPE LEO I, A.D. 442

"I am cheered by the purport of your letter, wherein you have not omitted to state that blessed Peter is the Chief of the Apostles and the Rock of faith, and have judiciously proved that to him were entrusted the keys of the heavenly mysteries."
                                        — POPE FELIX III, A.D. 490

Peter Is the Chief Shepherd of the Church

"When the Chief Authority as regards the feeding of the sheep was delivered to Peter; and on him, as on earth, the Church was founded; of no other virtue was the confession required, than that of love."   — ORIGEN, C. A.D. 216

"Peter, also to whom the Lord commends His sheep to be fed and guarded, on whom He laid the foundation of the Church."

— CYPRIAN, C. A.D. 246

"For He said to Simon Cephas, 'Feed My sheep and My lambs and My ewes.' So Simon fed His sheep, and he fulfilled his time and handed over the flock to you and departed."

— APHRAATES THE PERSIAN SAGE, C. A.D. 336

"He was the prince of the Apostles, and had received the keys, and was accounted the shepherd of the flock."

— EPHRAEM THE SYRIAN, C. A.D. 350-370

"After the Savior all were included in Peter; for He constituted him to be their head, that he might be the shepherd of the Lord's flock." — AMBROSIASTER, C. A.D. 380-384

"He heard from that same God: Peter, 'feed My lambs'; to him was entrusted the flock; he leads the way admirably in the power of his own Master." — EPIPHANIUS, C. A.D. 385

"Peter, after having been tempted by the devil, is set over the Church. The Lord, therefore, signified beforehand what that is, that He afterwards chose him the pastor of the Lord's flock. For to him He said, 'But thou, when thou art converted, confirm thy brethren.'" — AMBROSE, C. A.D. 385-389

"In those days Peter rose up in the midst of the disciples" (Acts 1:15): "Both as being ardent, and as entrusted by Christ with the flock, . . . he first acts with authority in this matter, as having all put into his hands; for to him Christ had said, 'And thou, being converted, confirm thy brethren." — JOHN CHRYSOSTOM, A.D. 387

"The Savior confided to this man, as some special trust, the whole Universal Church, after having asked him three times 'Do you love me?' And he received the world in charge, as one flock and one shepherd, having heard, 'Feed my lambs'; and the Lord gave, well nigh in his own stead, that most faithful disciple to the proselytes as a father, and shepherd and instructor." — ASTERIUS, A.D. 395

"Peter, to whom He commended His sheep as another self, He wished to make one with Himself, that so He might commend the sheep to him; that he might be the head, he bear the figure of the Body — that is, of the Church — and as husband and wife be two in one flesh."   — AUGUSTINE, C. A.D. 400

"He who was appointed shepherd of the Lord's sheep in perpetuity cannot but be very close to you, cannot but watch over any church, no matter where it is situated, in which we have laid a foundation stone of the Universal Church."
                              — POPE BONIFACE I, A.D. 419

"Peter found a grace greater than that which he had lost. As a good shepherd, he received the flock to guard, that he, who before had been weak in his own case, might become a support to all."
                              — MAXIMUS OF TURIN, A.D. 424

"He [Christ] promises to found the church, assigning immoveableness to it, as he is the Lord of strength, and over this he sets Peter as shepherd."   — CYRIL OF ALEXANDRIA, A.D. 429

"Hence, it is that, when about to return to heaven, He commends His sheep to be fed by Peter, in his Stead. Peter, says He, 'Do you love Me? Feed My sheep."   — PETER CHRYSOLOGUS, A.D. 432

"First He committed to him the lambs, then the sheep; because He constituted him not only shepherd, but the shepherd of shepherds. Therefore, Peter feeds the lambs, he feeds also the sheep; he feeds the offspring, he feeds also the mothers; he rules both subjects and prelates. He is the shepherd, therefore, of all, because, besides lambs and sheep, there is nothing in the Church."
— EUCHERIUS, C. A.D. 440

"Behold, that succor is given to a penitent Apostle, who is the Bishop of bishops, and a greater rank is restored to him now weeping than was taken from him when he 'denied.' That I may prove this, I show that no other Apostle received the name of Shepherd. For the Lord Jesus alone said, 'I am the Good Shepherd'; and again, 'My sheep,' He says, 'Follow Me.' This holy name, therefore, and the power of the same name, He, after the resurrection, conceded to the penitent Peter."
— ARNOBIUS JUNIOR, A.D. 440

"So this great pillar supported the tossing and sinking world, and permitted it not to fall entirely and gave it back stability, having been ordered to feed God's sheep." — THEODORET, C. A.D. 450

"[F]or not only was the power of binding and loosing given to Peter before the others, but also to Peter more especially was entrusted the care of feeding the sheep. Yet anyone who holds that the headship must be denied to Peter, cannot really diminish his dignity: but is puffed up with the breath of his pride, and plunges himself to the lowest depth."   — POPE LEO I, A.D. 450

"Him on whom the Lord enjoined the care of all the sheepfold."
— POPE SIMPLICIUS, A.D. 468

"And again to the same Peter, 'Lo! I have prayed for you that your faith fail not, and converted, confirm the brethren,' and that sentence, 'If you love Me, feed my sheep.' Wherefore, then, is the Lord's discourse so frequently directed to Peter?"

— POPE GELASIUS I, A.D. 492

Peter's Seat of Authority and Apostolic Succession

"Our apostles, too, were given to understand by our Lord Jesus Christ that the office of the bishop would give rise to intrigues. For this reason, equipped as they were with perfect foreknowledge, they appointed the men mentioned before, and afterwards laid down a rule once for all to this effect: when these men die, other approved men shall succeed to their sacred ministry."

— POPE CLEMENT I, A.D. 96

"On him He builds the Church, and to him He gives the command to feed the sheep; and although He assigns a like power to all the Apostles, yet He founded a single chair, and He established by His own authority a source and an intrinsic reason for that unity. Indeed, the others were that also which Peter was; but a primacy is given to Peter, whereby it is made clear that there is but one Church and one chair."   — CYPRIAN, C. A.D. 246

"He who so prides himself on the place of his episcopate, and contends that he holds the succession of Peter, upon whom the foundations of the Church were laid, introduces many other rocks . . . and sets up the new buildings of many Churches, while by his own authority he maintains that there is baptism among them."

— FIRMILIAN, C. A.D. 254

"There were both the prince of the Old and the prince of the New Testament confronting one another. There the saintly Moses beheld the sanctified Simon the steward of the Father, the procurator of the Son. He who forced the sea asunder to let the people walk across the parted waves, beheld him who raised the new tabernacle and built the Church."

— EPHRAEM THE SYRIAN, C. A.D. 350-370

". . . in which Chair unity should be preserved by all, so that he should now be schismatic and a sinner who should set up another Chair against that unique one. Therefore in the Single Chair, which is the first of the endowments sat first Peter, to whom succeeded Linus . . . to Damasus succeeded Siricius, who is our colleague, with whom the whole world together with us is united in one fellowship of communion by the interchange of letters."

— OPTATUS OF MILEVIS, C. A.D. 370

"Moses was succeeded by Peter, who had committed to his hands the new Church of Christ, and the true priesthood."

— MACARIUS OF EGYPT, A.D. 371

"I think it my duty to consult the chair of Peter, and to turn to a church whose faith has been praised by Paul. I appeal for spiritual food to the church whence I have received the garb of Christ."

— JEROME, C. A.D. 375

"It was right indeed that he [Paul] should be anxious to see Peter; for he was the first among the apostles, and was entrusted by the Savior with the care of the churches."

— AMBROSIASTER, C. A.D. 380-384

"Taking into account my office, it is not for me to choose — on whom it is incumbent that there should be a zeal for the Christian religion greater than that of all other persons — to dissemble, and remain silent. I bear the burdens of all who are heavily laden; yea,

rather in me that burden is borne by the blessed Apostle Peter, who
we trust, in all things, protects, and has regard to us who are the
heirs of his Government."
— POPE SIRICIUS, C. A.D. 384-386

"And should any one say, 'Why then did James receive the throne
of Jerusalem?': this is my answer: that He appointed this man
(Peter) not teacher of that throne, but of the habitable globe."
— JOHN CHRYSOSTOM, A.D. 387

"I am held in the communion of the Catholic Church by . . . the
succession of priests from the very Chair of the Apostle Peter, to
whom the Lord, after his resurrection, committed his sheep to be
fed, even to the present Episcopate." — AUGUSTINE, C. A.D. 400

"Possessing the first chair, he [Peter] throws open the gates of eternity, that have been entrusted to him." — PRUDENTIUS, A.D. 405

"Peter, through whom both the apostolate and episcopate took its
beginnings in Christ."   — POPE INNOCENT I, A.D. 410

"If, for one man's fault, the population of a whole province is to
be anathematized, then will be condemned also that most blessed
disciple (of Peter), Rome to wit, out of which there have sprung
up not one, but two or three, or even more heresies, and yet not
one of them has been able either to have possession, or to move the
Chair of Peter, that is, the Seat of Faith." — BACHIARIUS, A.D. 420

"You have learned by the result of this present business what it is
to agree in sentiment with us. The blessed Apostle Peter, in his
Successors, has transmitted what he received. Who would separate
himself from his doctrine, whom the Master Himself declared to
be the First among the Apostles?" — POPE SIXTUS III, A.D. 434

"But this man will not abide by the decrees (of Nicea), but brings forward at every turn that his is the throne of Mark; and yet he knows well that the great city of Antioch has the throne of Peter, who was both the teacher of Mark, and the first and the leader (coryphaeus) of the choir of the Apostles."

— THEODORET, C. A.D. 450

"This same norm of apostolic doctrine persists in the successors of him to whom the Lord enjoined the care of the entire sheepfold."

— POPE SIMPLICIUS, A.D. 468

Peter and the Primacy of Rome

"The Church of God which sojourns at Rome, to the Church of God sojourning at Corinth, to them that are called and sanctified by the will of God, through our Lord Jesus Christ: Grace to you, and peace, from Almighty God through Jesus Christ, be multiplied. Owing to the suddenly bursting and rapidly succeeding calamities and untoward experiences that have befallen us, we have been somewhat tardy; we think, in giving our attention to the subjects of dispute in your community, beloved.... Receive our counsel, and ye shall have no occasion of regret.... For ye will give us great joy and gladness, if ye render obedience unto the things written by us through the Holy Spirit, and root out the unrighteous anger of your jealousy, according to the entreaty which we have made for peace and concord in this letter." — POPE CLEMENT I, A.D. 96

"Ignatius, also called Theophorus, to the Church that has found mercy in the transcendent Majesty of the Most High Father and of Jesus Christ, His only Son; the church by the will of Him who willed all things that exist, beloved and illuminated through the faith and love of Jesus Christ our God; which also presides in the chief place of the Roman territory; a church worthy of God, worthy of honor, worthy of felicitation, worthy of praise, worthy of success, worthy of sanctification, and presiding in love, maintaining the law of Christ. . . . You have never grudged any man. You have taught others."   — IGNATIUS, A.D. 107

"Rome is called, 'The Apostolic throne.'"
                    — ATHANASIUS, A.D. 362

"The faith (of Rome) was of old, and still is now, right, binding the whole West by the saving word, as is just in her who presides over all, reverencing the whole harmonious teaching of God."
                    — GREGORY OF NAZIANZUS, C. A.D. 370

"You cannot deny that you know that in the city of Rome the Chair was first conferred on Peter, in which the prince of all the Apostles, Peter, sat."   — OPTATUS OF MILEVIS, C. A.D. 370

"We will that all people who are governed by our clemency should practice the same religion as the divine Apostle Peter delivered to the Romans, as the religion proclaimed by him up to this time declares it."   — THEODOSIUS I, A.D. 380

"We have considered that it ought to be announced that although all the Catholic Churches spread abroad through the world comprise but one bridal chamber of Christ, nevertheless, the holy Roman Church has been placed at the forefront not by the conciliar decisions of other Churches, but has received the primacy by the evangelic voice of our Lord and Savior, who says: 'You are Peter, and upon this rock I will build my Church. . . .' The first see, therefore, is that of Peter the Apostle, that of the Roman Church, which has neither stain nor blemish nor anything like it."
                    — POPE DAMASUS I, A.D. 382

"St. Ambrose . . . declares union with the Roman See to be union with the Catholic Church. Speaking of his brother Satyrus, who had arrived, after shipwreck, in a place of doubtful orthodoxy, he says: 'He called the Bishop to him, and not accounting any grace true which was not of the true faith, he inquired of him whether he agreed with the Catholic Bishops, that is, with the Roman Church.' "   — AMBROSE, A.D. 385

"This is also one privilege of our city, that it received in the beginning for its teacher the chief of the Apostles. For it was befitting that city which, before the rest of the world, was crowned with the name of Christian, should receive as shepherd the first of the Apostles. But, after having had him as our teacher, we did not retain him, but surrendered him to Imperial Rome."
                                          — JOHN CHRYSOSTOM, A.D. 387

"Far be this from the Catholic discipline of the Roman Church. . . . Assuredly care shall not be wanting on my part to guard the faith of the Gospel for my people; and to visit by Letter, as far as I be able, the members of my body, throughout the divers regions of the earth, to prevent any beginning of a profane interpretation from creeping in, which may have for its object to confound devout minds, by spreading its darkness." — POPE ANASTASIUS I, A.D. 399

"To be unwilling to give the primacy [*primas*] to the Roman Church either stems from the utmost impiety or from rash arrogance."   — AUGUSTINE, C. A.D. 400

"For who knows not, or notices not, that what was delivered to the Roman Church by Peter, the Prince of the Apostles, and is to this day guarded, ought to be introduced which has not (that) authority, or which may seem to derive its precedent elsewhere."
                                          — POPE INNOCENT I, A.D. 410

"... Peter is a Head of such great authority, and that he has confirmed the subsequent decrees (or statutes) of the Fathers; that, by all laws and regulations, both human and divine, the Roman Church is strengthened; and you are not ignorant, you know, dearest brethren, and as priests you are not ignorant, that we rule over his Place, and are in possession also of the Authority of his name."   — POPE ZOSIMUS, A.D. 417

"I appeal to the justice of your Holiness, my Lord Zosimus, venerable Pope. The true faith is never troubled, and this especially in the Apostolic Church, wherein the teachers of a corrupt faith are as easily detected as they are truly punished ... that they may have in them that true faith which the Apostles taught, and which is held by the Roman Church, and by all the teachers of the Catholic faith."   — PAULINUS OROSIUS, A.D. 418

"Wherefore you shall execute this Judgment with the Authority of our See, acting in our Stead, and having our Power delegated to you; and that if, in the space of ten days after he (Nestorius) has received this admonition, he does not expressly anathematize his impious doctrines, and promise to confess for the future, that faith which the Roman Church and your Church and all Christendom teaching concerning the generation of Jesus Christ our God, your Holiness may forthwith set about to provide for this Church under the full assurance that in such a case it is necessary that he should be utterly separated from our body."
                                        — POPE CELESTINE I, C. A.D. 423

"The primacy of the Apostolic See having been established by the merit of the Apostle Peter, by dignity of the city of Rome, and by the authority of the Holy Synod, no pretended power shall arrogate to itself anything against the authority of that See. For peace can be universally preserved only when the whole Church acknowledges its ruler."   — VALENTINIAN III, A.D. 445

"We exhort you, honorable brother, that you obediently listen to what has been written by the blessed Pope of the city of Rome, since Blessed Peter, who lives and presides in his own see, offers the truth of faith to those who seek. For we, in our zeal for peace and faith, cannot decide questions of faith apart from the consent of the Bishop of Rome."　　— PETER CHRYSOLOGUS, A.D. 449

"As the most blessed Peter received the apostolic primacy from the Lord, and the Roman Church continues in his institutions, it is criminal to believe that his holy disciple, Mark, who was first that governed the church of Alexandria, formed decrees by other rules of his own traditions; since without doubt from the same source of grace was the spirit both of the disciple and of his master."

— POPE LEO I, C. A.D. 450

"Rome, the See of Peter, . . . made to the world the head of pastoral honor, possess by religion what it did not possess by arms."

— PROSPER OF ACQUITAINE, C. A.D. 450

"I, therefore, beseech your holiness to persuade the most holy and blessed Archbishop (Leo) to use his apostolic power, and to order me to hasten to your Council. . . . For that most holy throne [in Rome] has the sovereignty over the churches throughout the universe on many grounds."　　— THEODORET, C. A.D. 450

"The Roman Church, which is the head of all the churches."

— VICTOR OF VITA, A.D. 480

"Referring to the adjudication of the Primacy to Rome, he says, 'as being men who bore in mind the Lord's sentence, "You are Peter, and upon this rock I will build my Church, etc." And again to the same Peter, "Lo! I have prayed for you that your faith fail not, and converted, confirm thy brethren," and that sentence, "If you love Me, feed my sheep." ' "   — POPE GELASIUS I, A.D. 492

"You know that the Synodal laws have it that if any doubt arise in matters pertaining to the state of the Church, we have recourse to the Bishop of the Roman Church as to our head."
                                                    — AVITUS, C. A.D. 495.[3]

---

[3] The foregoing material was taken from the following resources: Colin Lindsay, *The Evidence for the Papacy* (London: Longmans, 1870); Dr. Hergenrother, *Anti-Janus: An Historico-Theological Criticism of the Work, Entitled 'The Pope and the Council,' By Janus* (Dublin: W.B. Kelly, 1870), Lat. trans. John Collorafi; J. Waterworth, *A Commentary by Writers of The First Five Centuries on the Place of St. Peter in the New Testament and that of St. Peter's Successors in the Church* (London: Thomas Richardson, 1871); Charles F.B. Allnatt, ed., *Cathedra Petri — The Titles and Prerogatives of St. Peter* (London: Burns & Oates, 1879); Joseph Berington, John Kirk, eds., and James Waterworth, rev., *The Faith of Catholics*, vol. 2, (New York: Pustet & Co., 1884); Luke Rivington, *The Primitive Church and the See of St. Peter* (London: Longmans, Green and Co., 1894); Dom John Chapman, *Bishop Gore and Catholic Claims* (London: Longmans, Green, and Co., 1905); S. Herbert Scott, *The Eastern Churches and the Papacy* (London: Sheed & Ward, 1928); *The Epistles of St. Clement of Rome and St. Ignatius of Antioch*, Ancient Christian Writers, (New York: Newman Press, 1946), trans. James A. Kleist; J.P. Migne, ed., *Patrologiae Cursus Completus: Series Graeca* (Paris, 1866, 40:273), in E. Giles, Documents Illustrating Papal Authority, A.D. 96-454, (London: SPCK, 1952); Michael M. Winter, *St. Peter and the Popes* (Baltimore: Helicon, 1960); W.A. Jurgens, *The Faith of the Early Fathers*, vol. 1, (Collegeville, MN: The Liturgical Press, 1970); Robert Murray, *Symbols of Church and Kingdom: A Study in Early Syriac Tradition* (London: Cambridge, 1975); *The Great Commentary of Cornelius Lapide*, II, Catholic Standard Library, trans. Mossman (John Hodges & Co, 1887), 220, in Michael Mallone, ed., *The Apostolic Digest* (Irving ,TX: Sacred Heart, 1987); Johannes Quasten, *Patrology*, (Westminster, MD: Christian Classics, 1993); Philip Schaff and Henry Wace, eds., *Nicene and Post-Nicene Fathers* (Peabody, MA: Hendrickson, 1994).

CHAPTER NINE

—⟶∿∿⟵—

No Salvation Outside the Church

This book has demonstrated from both Scripture and the early Church Fathers that Jesus Christ established the One, Holy, Catholic, and Apostolic Church upon the rock of Peter and his successors. Through the divine office of the papacy, Jesus has preserved the integrity of His saving Gospel throughout the ages and provided a single and visible source of unity for the worldwide family of God.

This book would not be complete without emphasizing the necessity for all men to be members of the Catholic Church to save their souls from eternal damnation. God desires all men to be saved, and Jesus Christ established the Catholic Church for the salvation of souls. Therefore, popes over the centuries, under the guidance of the Holy Spirit, have infallibly declared: "Outside the Church there is no salvation" (in Latin, *Extra ecclesiam nulla salus est*). We complete our study of the papacy by briefly exploring this dogmatic teaching.

Reformulated positively, this infallible dogma means that all salvation comes from Jesus Christ the Head through the Catholic Church, which is His body. As we have seen, this Church is both visible (pope, bishops, priests, and deacons) and invisible (the Mystical body of Christ). As with the unity of the visible human body and its invisible soul, there can be no unity in the Mystical body without unity in the visible body, the Church. Jesus provides this unity through His Vicar, the pope. Just as Jesus has redeemed us through the sacrifice of His physical body, He applies the fruits of His redemption to us through His Mystical body. As Paul says: "He is the saviour of his body" (Eph 5:23).

Because Jesus is the Savior of His body, one must be a member of this body to be saved. Jesus did not acquire the Church with His own blood[1] so that the Church would be optional. He did not create an office of Vicars to rule and govern His Church and teach with infallibility so that the Church would be dispensable. He did not promise that the gates of hell would never prevail against His Church so that we could be saved outside of her. Both Jesus Christ and the Catholic Church are objectively necessary for salvation.

This, however, does not mean that only Catholics will be saved. The Church allows for the possibility that some people may be saved without becoming formal members of the Catholic Church. This may happen by a special grace that God gives a person at death that moves him to make an act of faith and sufficient repentance for his sins. While such death-bed conversions are possible, it is believed that they are extremely rare.[2] There is an old Catholic maxim that says: "As you live, so you die."

The Church also acknowledges that a person may be invincibly ignorant of the need to join the Catholic Church through no fault of his own. God does not punish those who are not guilty of deliberate sin. In cases of invincible ignorance (for example, a person never heard the claims of Jesus Christ and the Catholic Church), those who seek God with a sincere heart and, moved by grace, try to do His will might also achieve eternal salvation. Their faith, hope, and charity can bring them, however imperfectly, into communion with the Catholic Church, the only ark of salvation.

Nevertheless, being invincibly ignorant of the truth of Jesus Christ is an undesirable position in which to be. Those who are out-

---

[1] See Acts 20:28.

[2] Jerome, the translator of the Latin Vulgate, believed that such conversions happen once in every 200,000 deaths.

side the Church may have the possibility of salvation, but this does not necessarily mean a "probability," or even a "good possibility." Jesus said: "I am the way, and the truth, and the life. No man cometh to the Father, but by me" (Jn 14:6). Peter also revealed: "Neither is there salvation in any other. For there is no other name under heaven given to men, whereby we must be saved" (Acts 4:12).

The Church has condemned the error that one should have the good hope of eternal salvation for all those who have never lived in the true Church of Christ. Such a mentality would threaten the Church's divine mission and foster the heresy of indifferentism. Moreover, those outside the Church lack the objective means by which Christ saves sinners — namely, through the seven sacraments and the teachings of the infallible Magisterium.

The Church does not make these ostensibly harsh judgments with an attitude of triumphalism. She does so out of love and zeal for souls, in obedience to her Founder's great commission: "Go ye into the whole world, and preach the gospel to every creature. He that believeth and is baptized, shall be saved: but he that believeth not shall be condemned" (Mk 16:15-16).

We are thus compelled by charity to refute the error of those who promote invincible ignorance as the gateway to a "universal salvation." Ignorance does not enable salvation; it only mitigates culpability. While non-Catholic religions may express a ray of truth that can enlighten men, it is erroneous to believe that all religions are more or less good and praiseworthy and offer man a way to be saved. If that were true, then the Son of God would not have had to become man, sacrificed Himself for the remission of our sins, and established a Church in His own blood. And He would not have declared to be the only way to the Father.

With our twenty-first-century technology, the Catholic Gospel is being transmitted to the far ends of the earth more than ever before through satellite and the Internet. As a result, hundreds of millions of non-Catholics know the claims of Christ and the

Catholic Church and, sadly, *still refuse to accept the invitation.* Many such people resist the grace of God, who wills all to be saved and come to the knowledge of the truth. Instead, many choose to persist in their errors and remain in their sinful lifestyles. We commend these people to the mercy of God, for these are the "other sheep" whom the Good Shepherd seeks to draw into the one fold of the Catholic Church (see Jn 10:16).

When God judges those who pass from this life without the Catholic faith, He takes into account all of the relevant facts and circumstances (for example, if they were ever presented the Gospel; if they investigated the Church; etc.). Only God knows whether a person is invincibly ignorant of the true faith. Only He can understand the minds, hearts, and thoughts of men. As Jeremiah says: "The heart is perverse above all things, and unsearchable, who can know it?" (Jer 17:9). We must never forget that God's mercy is as infinite as His justice.

Catholics, who have been baptized into the true faith and given the ordinary means of salvation (which is always by God's grace and no merit of their own), have a particular duty toward God and neighbor. Jesus said: "And unto whomsoever much is given, of him much shall be required" (Lk 12:48). With greater blessings come greater responsibilities. Those Catholics who have been faithful to the teachings of Christ and His Church can have a moral certitude of their salvation.

However, those Catholics who have separated themselves from the body through deliberate sin or disobedience will be judged more harshly than those who never knew Christ or His Church. Peter says: "For if, flying from the pollutions of the world, through the knowledge of our Lord and Saviour Jesus Christ, they be again entangled in them and overcome: their latter state is become unto them worse than the former" (2 Pet 2:20).

We dare not judge or prognosticate about the eternal fate of anyone. We are all in this journey together. The Church warns her members not to preoccupy themselves with speculation about the fate of those outside the Church as they attend to their needs with Christian charity and guide them back to Catholic truth. We must evangelize all men, work out our own salvation with "fear and trembling,"[3] and leave the rest to our merciful Lord. We will accomplish these divine tasks by trusting in the promises of Jesus, holding fast to the unity of Peter, and faithfully living the teachings of the Catholic Church, "the pillar and ground of the truth" (1 Tim 3:15).

Following are the teachings of the successors of Peter on the dogma "*Extra ecclesiam nulla salus est.*"[4]

—~~~—

"Consider the fact that whoever has not been in the peace and unity of the Church cannot have the Lord. . . . Although given over to flames and fires, they burn, or, thrown to wild beasts, they lay down their lives, there will not be (for them) that crown of faith but the punishment of faithlessness. . . . Such a one can be slain, he cannot be crowned. . . . [If] slain outside the Church, he cannot attain the rewards of the Church." — POPE PELAGIUS II (62ND SUCCESSOR TO PETER), DENZINGER 246-247, C. A.D. 579-590

"Now the holy Church universal proclaims that God cannot be truly worshipped, saving from within herself, asserting that all they that are without her shall never be saved."
— POPE ST. GREGORY THE GREAT (63RD SUCCESSOR TO PETER), *MORALIA IN IOB*, XIV:5, C. A.D. 590

---

[3] See Phil 2:12.
[4] The following passages are from the Vatican website, www.vatican.va.

"There is but one universal Church of the faithful, outside which no one at all is saved." — POPE INNOCENT III (175TH SUCCESSOR TO PETER), FOURTH LATERAN COUNCIL, A.D. 1215

"We declare, say, define, and pronounce that it is absolutely necessary for the salvation of every human creature to be subject to the Roman Pontiff." — POPE BONIFACE VIII (192ND SUCCESSOR TO PETER), BULL, *UNAM SANCTAM*, A.D. 1302

"The most Holy Roman Church firmly believes, professes, and preaches that none of those existing outside the Catholic Church, not only pagans, but also Jews and heretics and schismatics, can have a share in life eternal; but that they go into the eternal fire which was prepared for the devil and his angels, unless before death they are joined with her; and that so important is the unity of the ecclesiastical body that only those remaining within this unity can profit by the sacraments of the Church unto salvation, and they alone can receive an eternal recompense for their fasts, their almsgivings, their other works of Christian piety and the duties of a Christian soldier. No one, let his almsgiving be as great as it may, no one, even if he pour out his blood for the Name of Christ, can be saved, unless he remain within the bosom and the unity of the Catholic Church." — POPE EUGENE IV (206TH SUCCESSOR TO PETER), BULL, *CANTATE DOMINO*, A.D. 1442

"We profess that there is no salvation outside the Church . . . the Church is the pillar and firmament of truth, as the apostle Paul teaches (1 Tim 3). In reference to these words St. Augustine says: 'Whoever is without the Church will not be reckoned among the sons, and whoever does not want to have the Church as mother will not have God as Father.' "   — POPE LEO XII (251ST SUCCESSOR TO PETER), ENCYCLICAL, *UBI PRIMUM*, A.D. 1825

"The people must be assured, Venerable Brethren, that the profession of the Catholic Faith is alone the true one, since the Apostle tells us that there is one Lord and one baptism. As Jerome says, the man who eats the lamb outside of this house is profane, and the man who is not in the ark of Noe is going to perish in the deluge. Neither is there any other name apart from the name of Jesus Christ given to men by which we must be saved."   — POPE PIUS VIII (252ND SUCCESSOR TO PETER), ENCYCLICAL, *TRADITI HUMILITATI NOSTRAE*, A.D. 1829

"The holy universal Church teaches that it is not possible to worship God truly except in her (the Catholic Church); all who are outside her will not be saved."   — POPE GREGORY XVI (253RD SUCCESSOR TO PETER), ENCYCLICAL, *SUMMO IUGITER STUDIO*, A.D. 1832

"It must be held as a matter of faith that outside the Apostolic Roman Church, no one can be saved; that this is the only ark of salvation; that he who shall not have entered therein will perish in the flood."   — BLESSED POPE PIUS IX (254TH SUCCESSOR TO PETER), ALLOCUTION, *SINGULARI QUADAM*, A.D. 1854

"This is our last lesson to you; receive it, engrave it in your minds, all of you: by God's commandment salvation is to be found nowhere but in the Church."   — POPE LEO XIII (255TH SUCCESSOR TO PETER), ENCYCLICAL, *ANNUM INGRESSI SUMUS*, A.D. 1902

"Outside the true Church are: infidels, Jews, heretics, apostates, schismatics, and excommunicated persons. . . . No one can be saved outside the Catholic, Apostolic and Roman Church, just as no one could be saved from the flood outside the Ark of Noah, which was a figure of the Church."

— CATECHISM OF POPE ST. PIUS X
(256TH SUCCESSOR TO PETER), A.D. 1903-1914

"Such is the nature of the Catholic faith that it does not admit of more or less, but must be held as a whole, or as a whole rejected: This is the Catholic faith, which unless a man believe faithfully and firmly, he cannot be saved." — POPE BENEDICT XV
(257TH SUCCESSOR TO PETER),
ENCYCLICAL, *AD BEATISSIMI APOSTOLORUM*, A.D. 1914

"The Catholic Church alone is keeping the true worship. This is the font of truth, this is the house of faith, this is the temple of God; if any man enter not here, or if any man go forth from it, he is a stranger to the hope of life and salvation. . . . Furthermore, in this one Church of Christ, no man can be or remain who does not accept, recognize, and obey the authority and supremacy of Peter and his legitimate successors."   — POPE PIUS XI
(258TH SUCCESSOR TO PETER),
ENCYCLICAL, *MORTALIUM ANIMOS*, A.D. 1928

"By divine mandate the interpreter and guardian of the Scriptures, and the depository of Sacred Tradition living within her, the Church alone is the entrance to salvation: She alone, by herself, and under the protection and guidance of the Holy Spirit, is the source of truth."   — POPE PIUS XII (259TH SUCCESSOR TO PETER),
ALLOCUTION TO THE GREGORIAN, A.D. 1953

"Basing itself upon Sacred Scripture and Tradition, it [the Council] teaches that the Church, now sojourning on earth as an exile, is necessary for salvation. Christ, present to us in His Body, which is the Church, is the one Mediator and the unique way of salvation. In explicit terms He Himself affirmed the necessity of faith and baptism and thereby affirmed also the necessity of the Church, for through baptism as through a door men enter the Church. Whosoever, therefore, knowing that the Catholic Church was made necessary by Christ, would refuse to enter or to remain in it, could not be saved."   — POPE PAUL VI (261ST SUCCESSOR TO PETER), SECOND VATICAN COUNCIL, DOGMATIC CONSTITUTION ON THE CHURCH, *LUMEN GENTIUM*, A.D. 1964

—⁓⁓—

The Popes of the Catholic Church[1]

No.	Name	Reigned From	Reigned To
1.	St. Peter	33	67
2.	St. Linus	67	76
3.	St. Anacletus (Cletus)	76	88
4.	St. Clement I	88	97
5.	St. Evaristus	97	105
6.	St. Alexander I	105	115
7.	St. Sixtus I — also called Xystus I	115	125
8.	St. Telesphorus	125	136
9.	St. Hyginus	136	140
10.	St. Pius I	140	155
11.	St. Anicetus	155	166
12.	St. Soter	166	175
13.	St. Eleutherius	175	189
14.	St. Victor I	189	199
15.	St. Zephyrinus	199	217
16.	St. Callistus I	217	222
17.	St. Urban I	222	230
18.	St. Pontain	230	235

---

[1] Adapted from the *Catholic Encyclopedia*, copyright 1913 by the Encyclopedia Press, Inc.

No.	Name	Reigned From	Reigned To
19.	St. Anterus	235	236
20.	St. Fabian	236	250
21.	St. Cornelius	251	253
22.	St. Lucius I	253	254
23.	St. Stephen I	254	257
24.	St. Sixtus II	257	258
25.	St. Dionysius	260	268
26.	St. Felix I	269	274
27.	St. Eutychian	275	283
28.	St. Caius — also called Gaius	283	296
29.	St. Marcellinus	296	304
30.	St. Marcellus I	308	309
31.	St. Eusebius	309	310
32.	St. Miltiades	311	314
33.	St. Sylvester I	314	335
34.	St. Marcus	336	336
35.	St. Julius I	337	352
36.	Liberius	352	366
37.	St. Damasus I	366	383
38.	St. Siricius	384	399
39.	St. Anastasius I	399	401
40.	St. Innocent I	401	417
41.	St. Zosimus	417	418
42.	St. Boniface I	418	422
43.	St. Celestine I	422	432
44.	St. Sixtus III	432	440

No.	Name	Reigned From	Reigned To
45.	St. Leo I (the Great)	440	461
46.	St. Hilarius	461	468
47.	St. Simplicius	468	483
48.	St. Felix III (II)	483	492
49.	St. Gelasius I	492	496
50.	Anastasius II	496	498
51.	St. Symmachus	498	514
52.	St. Hormisdas	514	523
53.	St. John I	523	526
54.	St. Felix IV (III)	526	530
55.	Boniface II	530	532
56.	John II	533	535
57.	St. Agapetus I — also called Agapitus I	535	536
58.	St. Silverius	536	537
59.	Vigilius	537	555
60.	Pelagius I	556	561
61.	John III	561	574
62.	Benedict I	575	579
63.	Pelagius II	579	590
64.	St. Gregory I (the Great)	590	604
65.	Sabinian	604	606
66.	Boniface III	607	607
67.	St. Boniface IV	608	615
68.	St. Deusdedit (Adeodatus I)	615	618
69.	Boniface V	619	625
70.	Honorius I	625	638

No.	Name	Reigned From	Reigned To
71.	Severinus	640	640
72.	John IV	640	642
73.	Theodore I	642	649
74.	St. Martin I	649	655
75.	St. Eugene I	655	657
76.	St. Vitalian	657	672
77.	Adeodatus (II)	672	676
78.	Donus	676	678
79.	St. Agatho	678	681
80.	St. Leo II	682	683
81.	St. Benedict II	684	685
82.	John V	685	686
83.	Conon	686	687
84.	St. Sergius I	687	701
85.	John VI	701	705
86.	John VII	705	707
87.	Sisinnius	708	708
88.	Constantine	708	715
89.	St. Gregory II	715	731
90.	St. Gregory III	731	741
91.	St. Zachary	741	752
92.	Stephen II — died before being consecrated	752	752
92.	Stephen III	752	757
93.	St. Paul I	757	767
94.	Stephen IV	767	772
95.	Adrian I	772	795

No.	Name	Reigned From	Reigned To
96.	St. Leo III	795	816
97.	Stephen V	816	817
98.	St. Paschal I	817	824
99.	Eugene II	824 ·	827
100.	Valentine	827	827
101.	Gregory IV	827	844
102.	Sergius II	844	847
103.	St. Leo IV	847	855
104.	Benedict III	855	858
105.	St. Nicholas I (the Great)	858	867
106.	Adrian II	867	872
107.	John VIII	872	882
108.	Marinus I	882	884
109.	St. Adrian III	884	885
110.	Stephen VI	885	891
111.	Formosus	891	896
112.	Boniface VI	896	896
113.	Stephen VII	896	897
114.	Romanus	897	897
115.	Theodore II	897	897
116.	John IX	898	900
117.	Benedict IV	900	903
118.	Leo V	903	903
119.	Sergius III	904	911
120.	Anastasius III	911	913
121.	Lando	913	914

No.	Name	Reigned From	Reigned To
122.	John X	914	928
123.	Leo VI	928	928
124.	Stephen VIII	929	931
125.	John XI	931	935
126.	Leo VII	936	939
127.	Stephen IX	939	942
128.	Marinus II	942	46
129.	Agapetus II	946	955
130.	John XII	955	963
131.	Leo VIII	963	964
132.	Benedict V	964	964
133.	John XIII	965	972
134.	Benedict VI	973	974
135.	Benedict VII	974	983
136.	John XIV	983	984
137.	John XV	985	996
138.	Gregory V	996	999
139.	Sylvester II	999	1003
140.	John XVII	1003	1003
141.	John XVIII	1003	1009
142.	Sergius IV	1009	1012
143.	Benedict VIII	1012	1024
144.	John XIX	1024	1032
145.	Benedict IX	1032	1045
146.	Sylvester III	1045	1045
147.	Benedict IX	1045	1045

No.	Name	Reigned From	Reigned To
148.	Gregory VI	1045	1046
149.	Clement II	1046	1047
150.	Benedict IX	1047	1048
151.	Damasus II	1048	1048
152.	St. Leo IX	1049	1054
153.	Victor II	1055	1057
154.	Stephen X	1057	1058
155.	Nicholas II	1058	1061
156.	Alexander II	1061	1073
157.	St. Gregory VII	1073	1085
158.	Bl. Victor III	1086	1087
159.	Bl. Urban II	1088	1099
160.	Paschal II	1099	1118
161.	Gelasius II	1118	1119
162.	Callistus II	1119	1124
163.	Honorius II	1124	1130
164.	Innocent II	1130	1143
165.	Celestine II	1143	1144
166.	Lucius II	1144	1145
167.	Bl. Eugene III	1145	1153
168.	Anastasius IV	1153	1154
169.	Adrian IV	1154	1159
170.	Alexander III	1159	1181
171.	Lucius III	1181	1185
172.	Urban III	1185	1187
173.	Gregory VIII	1187	1187

No.	Name	Reigned From	Reigned To
174.	Clement III	1187	1191
175.	Celestine III	1191	1198
176.	Innocent III	1198	1216
177.	Honorius III	1216	1227
178.	Gregory IX	1227	1241
179.	Celestine IV	1241	1241
180.	Innocent IV	1243	1254
181.	Alexander IV	1254	1261
182.	Urban IV	1261	1264
183.	Clement IV	1265	1268
184.	Bl. Gregory X	1271	1276
185.	Bl. Innocent V	1276	1276
186.	Adrian V	1276	1276
187.	John XXI	1276	1277
188.	Nicholas III	1277	1280
189.	Martin IV	1281	1285
190.	Honorius IV	1285	1287
191.	Nicholas IV	1288	1292
192.	St. Celestine V	1294	1294
193.	Boniface VIII	1294	1303
194.	Bl. Benedict XI	1303	1304
195.	Clement V	1305	1314
196.	John XXII	1316	1334
197.	Benedict XII	1334	1342
198.	Clement VI	1342	1352
199.	Innocent VI	1352	1362

No.	Name	Reigned From	Reigned To
200.	Bl. Urban V	1362	1370
201.	Gregory XI	1370	1378
202.	Urban VI	1378	1389
203.	Boniface IX	1389	1404
204.	Innocent VII	1406	1406
205.	Gregory XII	1406	1415
206.	Martin V	1417	1431
207.	Eugene IV	1431	1447
208.	Nicholas V	1447	1455
209.	Callistus III	1445	1458
210.	Pius II	1458	1464
211.	Paul II	1464	1471
212.	Sixtus IV	1471	1484
213.	Innocent VIII	1484	1492
214.	Alexander VI	1492	1503
215.	Pius III	1503	1503
216.	Julius II	1503	1513
217.	Leo X	1513	1521
218.	Adrian VI	1522	1523
219.	Clement VII	1523	1534
220.	Paul III	1534	1549
221.	Julius III	1550	1555
222.	Marcellus II	1555	1555
223.	Paul IV	1555	1559
224.	Pius IV	1559	1565
225.	St. Pius V	1566	1572

No.	Name	Reigned From	Reigned To
226.	Gregory XIII	1572	1585
227.	Sixtus V	1585	1590
228.	Urban VII	1590	1590
229.	Gregory XIV	1590	1591
230.	Innocent IX	1591	1591
231.	Clement VIII	1592	1605
232.	Leo XI	1605	1605
233.	Paul V	1605	1621
234.	Gregory XV	1621	1623
235.	Urban VIII	1623	1644
236.	Innocent X	1644	1655
237.	Alexander VII	1655	1667
238.	Clement IX	1667	1669
239.	Clement X	1670	1676
240.	Bl. Innocent XI	1676	1689
241.	Alexander VIII	1689	1691
242.	Innocent XII	1691	1700
243.	Clement XI	1700	1721
244.	Innocent XIII	1721	1724
245.	Benedict XIII	1724	1730
246.	Clement XII	1730	1740
247.	Benedict XIV	1740	1758
248.	Clement XIII	1758	1769
249.	Clement XIV	1769	1774
250.	Pius VI	1775	1799
251.	Pius VII	1800	1823

No.	Name	Reigned From	Reigned To
252.	Leo XII	1823	1829
253.	Pius VIII	1829	1830
254.	Gregory XVI	1831	1846
255.	Bl. Pius IX	1846	1878
256.	Leo XIII	1878	1903
257.	St. Pius X	1903	1914
258.	Benedict XV	1914	1922
259.	Pius XI	1922	1939
260.	Pius XII	1939	1958
261.	Bl. John XXIII	1958	1963
262.	Paul VI	1963	1978
263.	John Paul I	1978	1978
264.	John Paul II	1978	2005
265.	Benedict XVI	2005	

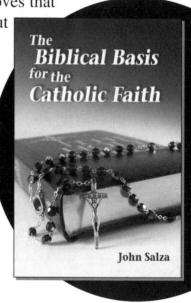